Northern Baja California
Mexico

Questions Answered by a Local Resident

Roberta Giesea

Script
STONE
PUBLISHING
HENDERSON, NV

© 1999 Roberta Giesea. All rights reserved.
No portion of this book may be reproduced or used in any form, or
by any means, without prior written permission of the publisher.

Script Stone Publishing
2675 Windmill Parkway, #612
Henderson, NV 89014 USA

First printing September 1999

10 9 8 7 6 5 4 3 2 1

Manufactured in the United States of America

Cover and Interior Design by Lightbourne

Library of Congress Catalog Card Number: 99-095013

ISBN: 0-9673647-3-6

DISCLAIMER

The author of this book is sharing information that is reliable but not
guaranteed. Phone numbers, quoted prices and legal regulations may
fluctuate and change with time. Business or professional services have
been selectively recommended, but the author has no responsibility for
their performance and in no way is associated with them. It is recommended that legal or professional assistance be obtained when making
business, financial or any other important decisions. Feedback from
readers is encouraged and welcomed.

ACKNOWLEDGMENTS

I wish to express gratitude to each person
who generously contributed information to
this book. May it be a guide to all who
come to Northern Baja California.

Muchas Gracias, mis amigos!

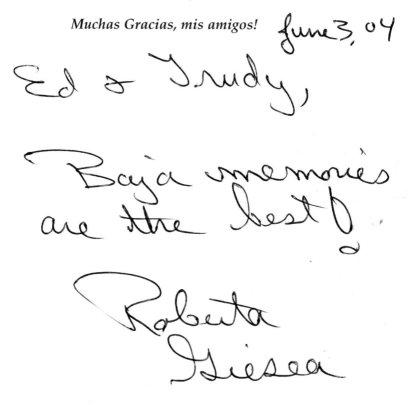

June 3, 04

Ed & Trudy,

Baja memories
are the best

Roberta
Giesea

AUTHOR PROFILE

Roberta Giesea trained as a high school English teacher before becoming a mother of five children. During her child-rearing days she co-authored books, *The Family Idea Book, Volumes I and II*, published by Deseret Books, that were designed to help parents raise children. She entered into the real estate field and became a top producer for Re/Max, winning awards given to those who are in the top one percent of the industry. Mexican vacations in Northern Baja California drew her permanently to that area where her passion for writing books was rekindled. "I enjoy living in a foreign country, especially on the beach where the sun shines," she says about her life in Mexico. "The Mexican people have an attitude about life that I admire. If this book can help those who visit or move here understand in a practical way how to live here, the bonus of appreciation for the culture will naturally follow."

CONTENTS

If this guidebook is used as a resource for answering questions as they arise, it will become a tattered, treasured friend.

INTRODUCTION

Bienvenidos, mis amigos! Welcome, my friends! You are about to sit at my kitchen table for an informative discussion concerning a topic that mutually interests us. You will ask me questions about living in Baja California, and I will answer them as succinctly as possible. My answers are generally objective, but some are subjective according to my personal perceptions and opinions. They will be sprinkled with anecdotes from my personal journal, so be prepared to taste life in Baja California through my eyes as I experience it. I will also introduce you to some of my friends. You will be able to view Baja California through their eyes as well. I've tried to anticipate your questions, but if I've missed something important, please give me feedback. I'm open to discussion and will revise my perceptions or answers as needed.

The purpose of our discussion is twofold. The first is to be a resource of practical knowledge concerning life in Baja California, including Tijuana and Ensenada with concentration on the Rosarito Beach area. If you're interested in another area of Mexico, you'll find the answers to many questions applicable, so don't feel you have to leave my kitchen table. Many of my answers will help you too. The first few months of living in a foreign country offer challenges of a cultural change. In this discussion, I'm your guide. I will patiently do my part in the discussion. I hope you will do yours, which is not only to have an open mind to receive the information but to have an open heart to feel the warmth and beauty of the culture we're discussing. If I help to foster a love and appreciation which causes your heart to beat in *simpatica* or harmony with the culture, then I've reached my goal in taking time to sit at my table to talk to you, my reader.

Salud! We are *Paisanos,* compatriots, of two wonderful countries. Let us begin.

Moonlight Pathway

Full moon last night glistening like a shimmering pathway on the ocean. It is a time for lovers to caressingly linger in the moonlight, for poets to pen heartfelt sonnets and for singers to passionately express their deepest sentiments. Enchanting, romantic, rapturous and captivating is this magic moment in Baja California.

A spirit of love and caring is in the air. Everyone should breathe in their share, savor it, and then exhale their own uniqueness, thus adding to the whole. Here in Baja California time stands still. *El corazon,* the heart, rules. There is no hurry. There is no frenzy.
There is no rat race.

But there is the pathway to the moon dancing on the surface of the Pacific. It is mine to relish in the middle of the night. . . . It could be yours as well. . . . **Where are you?**

—Roberta Giesea

CHAPTER ONE

BAJA CALIFORNIA

. . . una isla como una leyenda de fantasía . . .
. . . an island like a fantasy legend . . .
—Martin Barron E., Guia
Historica de Baja California

What is the difference between Baja California and Baja California Sur?

The Mexican peninsula south of San Diego, California and west of the Sea of Cortez is divided into two states, **Baja California Norte** and **Baja California Sur, Mexico**. Both are separated from the mainland of Mexico by the Sea of Cortez and total approximately one thousand miles in length.

Although the north and south have much in common, Northern Baja California has a distinct identity which separates it from its southern counterpart. The northern area, Baja California Norte, which stops at the 28th Parallel just north of Guerrero Negro, is considered to be the "border area," influenced by the American culture found heavily in Tijuana and Rosarito but diminishing as one travels southward. Each state has its own governor and representatives. Baja California Norte is often called Baja California without the Norte; thus many references in this book will drop the Norte, referring to the northern state as merely Baja California. It has a much larger population than its southern counterpart.

Why is this part of Mexico called Baja California?

Don't make the mistake of calling this lovely Mexican area **Baja**. *Baja* is Spanish for lower. The proper name is Baja California. It isn't just lower; it is Lower California, Mexico. After all, it is the original California, which under Mexico included the vast northern territory, now fragmented into different countries. The upper part, now the state of California USA, was officially ceded to the United States when the treaty of Guadalupe Hidalgo was signed on February 2, 1848, ending the Mexican-American War (1846-1848). The Mexicans feel their land was "stolen" from them; so when it's referred to as merely Baja, it's an added insult.

At least three versions of the origin of the name exist, one more romantic than the other. The first is that the Spanish explorer, Hernán Cortés, used the words, *Cálida Fornax*, translated, "hot furnace", to describe the area after an expedition in 1535. Through the years those words eventually changed to California.

The other, more romantic version, is attributed to a narrative written by Garci Ordonez de Montalvo in 1510 entitled *Las Sergas de Esplandian* or *The Exploits of Esplandian,* in which there is a queen named Calafia who ruled a band of female warriors on a mysterious gold-rich island. The description of the island's terrain resembles that of the peninsula of Baja California. Cortés also described the strong race who lived there as beautiful with naked bodies adorned with *perlas de gran tamaño* or pearls of great size. As a result, the area was considered to be *una isla como una leyenda de fantasía* or an island like a fantasy legend. It is interesting to note that it was believed to be an island until between 1699 and 1702 a Jesuit missionary proved it could be reached by land by various expeditions. Needless to say, the name Calafia, attributed to a lovely warrior queen who defended riches beyond comprehension with her band of female followers, sounds like an imaginative explanation that is as plausible as any other.

Thirdly, interesting to note that the Spanish word *cala* means "cove" in English. Perhaps the derivative of the name California is from the root word *cala* or "cove", which would describe most of the Baja California coastline.

Speaking of the word Calafia, it is the name of a famous old mission which is now a resort located six miles south of Rosarito on the free road. It not only offers a popular restaurant-hotel with fantastic ocean views, but the historic exhibitions are enriching to those who enjoy history. I was standing on Calafia's deck which overhangs the ocean when I witnessed a migrating whale soar through the air in an amazing arc. This is a spot where the blue waters of the Pacific can be relished with the dignity they deserve.

What is the *Baja rapture*?

When emotions of compelling love for Baja California take over reason, it is called **Baja rapture**. It enters your heart unexpectedly for any number of reasons. Be careful! If it targets you, you may fall under its magnetic pull and you may become my neighbor.

The following incident relates such a pull on my soul:

> Just before sunrise I left the comfort of my bedroom to venture out to the sandy beach that is the daily recipient of treasures deposited overnight by saltwater waves from places unknown. With the anticipation of acquiring new additions to my shell collection, I walked the beach in solitude. As I strolled along slowly combing the sand at the water line with my eyes, my mind was far away contemplating a serious problem I needed to resolve. I was so absorbed in myself, I at first failed to notice a dark-haired boy dressed in shorts and a T-shirt who wandered out of a waterfront shanty with his dog trotting by his side. He shyly smiled, answering timidly when I asked him how old he was. He said he was nine years old. He then ran back into his house, leaving me wondering if my illiterate attempt at speaking Spanish had scared him off. Evidently he was not afraid, because he returned in a few minutes with a portable radio blaring Mexican music. He placed it carefully in my hands. He then turned away from me to walk the beach with his dog, leisurely looking for treasures. On his return, he handed me a perfectly sculptured shell that was obviously the former home of a sea snail. As I turned it over to study it, he grinned with pleasure. It was in perfect condition. His black

eyes were full of an innocent, twinkling light that penetrated into my heart, magically evaporating any preoccupation I had with personal problems. I knew I had made a friend. I smiled for the first time in days as I returned his radio to him. I thanked him in Spanish with a heart touched by a friendly moment in Baja California. Now, weeks later, I recall a simple connection with a little Mexican boy each time I look at the white shell in my garden collection. In its intricate formation of spirals created by Mother Nature, it reflects only a part of the Baja California beauty. The fact that it now adorns my garden as a gift from a little Mexican boy reflects the deeper pull of the Baja California spell. That little boy so full of simple kindness holds the secret of Baja rapture. Perhaps, in his innocence, he holds the secret of life.

The following is from the Internet site, www.bajanet.com, written by Divrdan who obviously has visited Baja California over the years but has not yet moved here. Although he refers to it as the **Baja bug**, it's similar but maybe not as intense as what others refer to as Baja rapture:

Baja bug is "an ailment most of the rest of us caught after our first visit down there anywhere from one to fifty years ago. At least once a year you develop the uncontrollable urge to have fine dust fill all the nooks and crannies of you and your vehicle while carelessly bounding down unpaved and previously unexplored 'roads' across the desert, or to stand in very warm clear water on endless white sand beaches with a fishing pole in your grasp, or fall asleep at night watching more stars than you thought could exist while listening to tiny Gulf wavelets slap the shore, or sit at an open air café eating fish tacos and swilling Pacificos while talking to strangers in a foreign tongue—and so on. The odds are pretty good that you'll catch it, and from then on work to feed the bug. We really are the lucky ones!"

The difference between the rapture and bug must be intensity because he's not living here yet, but he's definitely under Baja California's magical spell. It hits each person differently, but the result is the same. A strong appreciation and desire to partake in the magical influence of the area overwhelms reason and usually wins.

Example of Baja rapture as quoted from my journal:

> Dick, let's move to Baja California, Mexico. Our dream can become a reality. So what if we leave our jobs behind and we have another ten years before retirement. Let's give up the rat race for a simpler life. Let's have faith in ourselves enough to walk off the edge into the unknown. We can find a new way to make money that will not be so demanding. If we don't do it now, we'll never do it.

Later, I wrote:

> Each time I'd return to Oregon to visit, I was miserable, especially when the weather was rainy and gloomy. The rush of life would get me down. However, the moment I crossed the border into Mexico on my return, I'd smile with anticipation while my heart rate increased with excitement. The burdens of life in the States melted away with each mile as I traveled toward my home in Mexico. There's something about the ocean, the sun and the air. It's a pull of a simpler life that says, "You're home. This is where you belong." If I

die in Mexico, I want my tombstone to read, "She died living her dream."

If I live in a border town will I miss the true Baja California experience?

There is no doubt the towns of Tijuana and Rosarito have not only benefited economically but have been contaminated culturally as the result of border proximity. However, to think the Mexican culture has been obliterated is ludicrous. The Cultural Center in downtown Tijuana reflects the culture formally, while it flourishes informally in the homes, schools and hearts of the local people. Many are drawn to American ways and have become affluent enough to form a middle class, but so far it has not been a detriment. The young people, as shown in the following journal excerpt, are being drawn to American ways:

> Saturday evening I visited the new AM/PM mini mart in Rosarito which was completed about three weeks ago. The clean, beautifully constructed building, located in a prominent site with entrances and exits on both the pay and free roads, is obviously an American icon and was placed there by no accident. It's the first retail American franchise to be built in Rosarito, unless one considers the Marriott Hotel north of town a retail franchise. The grand opening has come and gone, but it's obvious the patrons don't know it. I was amazed to see Mexican young people hanging out. They were clean, bright eyed and full of energy. Some were sitting at little round white tables drinking soft drinks, while others were surveying the array of American products that filled the shelves. Mostly they were in small groups

buzzing with excited conversations. As I watched, cars pulled up with still more young people, reminding me of my innocent teenage escapades at a local drive-in restaurant so many years ago. These young people were happily sharing their time with one another in "an American establishment." There were no spiked hair-dos or black leather outfits. There were no nose rings or tattoos. At first I was thrilled with their energy and excitement. Then a pang entered my heart because it was evident I was witnessing what the future will bring to Rosarito. A McDonald's will undoubtedly be next. This American establishment has already been added to Ensenada and Tijuana. Will American fads take over this youth? Oh, Mexico, beware. Let the heartbeat of your culture survive. Your strength lies in your spirituality and strong family values. Let these young people remain innocent and not yield to materialism. The treasures of your culture must prevail into the future.

Many people feel the true Baja California experience is to indulge in outdoor desert adventures. My question to them is, "Who's experiencing Baja California in depth? Those who travel through for a couple of weeks or months, or those who live in Baja California for years? Doesn't it make sense that if you live here you're available to indulge in all that's offered in the area all year round for years and years? Wouldn't residents of the area have more knowledge of the true Baja experience?"

I see a lot of shacks and business fronts that are junky. How could I consider living in such a town?

Two sayings apply to this observation. One is, "What you

see isn't always what you get." The other is, "Don't judge the inside by what you see on the outside." Like sea anemones, an inner beauty is protected from those who value different standards. Homes with brick or concrete fences that look plain on the outside could be masterpieces of taste on the inside. Makeshift shacks are homes of the poor, but these people have mansions compared to those with no homes at all. Look into the spirit that resides within and you'll see something far more valuable than you can imagine. Remember to keep an open mind as you travel from one culture to another.

My journal entry illustrates what a surprise can await when you enter into the world behind the streetfront façade:

> Today I decided to never judge a residence by its ordinary outside appearance. I've lived for a year across the street from a home that appears to be plainly enclosed within a white stucco fence that gives it an unimpressive appearance from the road. It looks like nothing special. When the owner invited me into his home for the first time today, I jumped at the opportunity. I discovered an estate that occupies eight lots, all overlooking the Pacific Ocean with magnificent terraces. The ocean is the backyard! A four-car garage, a fountain courtyard, a huge swimming pool and an outdoor bar are all outside within the high stucco walls. The house itself has a grand living room with a commanding view of the ocean. It's huge! The kitchen, entirely tiled from floor to ceiling, has all the modern conveniences anyone would enjoy. Words can't describe this breathtaking estate worth millions of dollars. No one would ever guess the grandeur behind the plain white walls is so uniquely impressive.

Jack Smith in a book titled *God and Mr. Gomez*, puts it as follows:

> Tijuana is easily scorned by more sophisticated travelers as a sleazy border town dusty trap of bad streets, girlie joints, pushers, panderers, and venal cops, all sicklied over with a shabbiness and poverty that shock Americans only minutes from the prosperous and tidy beach towns of California's south coast. Yet Tijuana exerts a magnetic pull on Americans and Mexicans alike, the first drawn by a taste for something foreign, the other by what is said to be the highest standard of living in Mexico. Tijuana claims, perhaps truthfully, to be the most visited city in the world.

Since Jack wrote those words, a lot of the sleazy entertainment has been cleaned up and the roads have been improved. New modern high rises can be found in the business section while an area called the *Playas*, or the beach, is similar to any California town. The strong magnetic power, however, is still present, luring many Americans to settle south of the border

Please note: New subdivisions built according to American standards are now available. They offer oceanfront homes with amenities such as tennis courts, swimming pools and weight rooms. One of the amenities is a sea anemone. Take time to study it down by the ocean with the wind in your hair while your toes wiggle in the sand. You may learn a secret too.

The land itself looks dry and barren.
Why would anyone go there?

If one could see dirt through the pavement of Los Angeles, California, he/she would discover that it is by nature a desolate land just as is Baja California, Mexico. Being a native of Los Angeles, I became a resident of Oregon's luscious greenery when I was eight years old so to me the words dry and barren pertain to the entire Southern California area. Water and civilization have changed it into a desirable residence for many people. Baja California, Mexico, has the same potential. The towns of Tijuana, Rosarito and Ensenada, which are the main focus of this book, offer many desirable areas in which to live. South of these border towns lie hundreds of miles of potential living area.

As one travels southward down the peninsula away from the border and Ensenada, civilization becomes sparser and sparser until it disappears completely. The road south of Ensenada has been paved since the 1970s, meandering inland from the ocean like a snake through desolate desert land filled with flat, dusty plateaus and towering rock formations. Water and gasoline become precious commodities in a land where there are no gas stations or roadside rest areas and few cars traveling in either direction. When other vehicles appear there's danger in passing, particularly when a bus, truck or RV is involved, because the road is a narrow, two-lane passage with no shoulders or guard rails to prevent tires from going off the road in a miscalculated attempt to pass. It's obvious that there are no hospitals or emergency vehicles to readily aid a victim of a car accident. This desert that appears on the surface to offer nothing to humans is really a land that is filled with rich treasures.

These treasures are hidden within the facade of desolation. Some are tangible goods such as onyx, marble, gold, or a rare goat-sheep that resides on rock mountains or whale-sharks that eat only plankton in the warm waters of the Sea of Cortéz. Other treasures are desert plants that offer unique medicinal properties that can be found nowhere else in the world. The richness of the land extends far beyond what the eye can see.

There are not enough words to describe the thrill of approaching the Sea of Cortez after driving ten hours through desert land of cactus and rock. A body of deep blue water appears to dazzle the eye amid so much dusty brown arid land. Something called appreciation for nature clicks within the soul, stirring feelings that can't be expressed adequately in any language. I imagine it's similar to the sentiments our pioneer ancestors had when they finally arrived, tired, dusty and road-weary in covered wagons at the place chosen for settlement.

What type of person discovers the beauty inside the protective appearance?

Mexico is not for everyone. The rugged lovers of the adventurous outdoors have touted the Baja California peninsula for years, but in recent times, retirees and vacationers have discovered it as a haven to suit their needs. Since the NAFTA agreement was signed, a different type of person has been drawn to Mexico. These are business people. They may be commuters who work in the San Diego area but live in Mexico, or they may be staffing such enterprises as the Fox Studio, Sharp Electronics or heading a *maquiladora* within the country. (See page 144 on business in Mexico.)

What are the misconceptions that prevent some people from moving to Mexico?

If I had listened to the following warnings, I never would have made the plunge to leave my home in Oregon for the richness of life in Baja California, Mexico:

♦ The police will hurt you.

♦ Con men will sell you worthless property.

♦ Crime is rampant—you'll get killed.

♦ Banks will fail and you'll lose everything.

♦ Roads are bad and driving conditions are impossible.

♦ Mexicans are bad people.

♦ The food and water will make you sick.

So many people have misconceptions about living in Mexico. It takes those who have an adventurous and open-minded spirit to see the truthful reality that will overcome these objections. How sad that untruths have so much control over the lives of those who don't do thorough research. Each of these topics will be addressed in this book. Hopefully, insight and knowledge will replace fear in making lifetime decisions.

C H A P T E R   T W O

TIJUANA, ROSARITO & ENSENADA

**Come, my friends, 'tis not too late
to seek a newer world.**
—Alfred Lord Tennyson

What are the advantages of choosing Northern Baja California, Mexico as a residence?

The US border is only minutes from Tijuana, one-half hour from Rosarito, and one hour from Ensenada. What does this mean?

♦ Visiting with friends and relatives from the States is

easy, since the San Diego airport is within an hour's commute. Travel time and expense are minimized into a reasonable framework in comparison to other areas of Mexico. For those who say, "I can't leave my children or grandchildren," the response is, "Let your children or grandchildren fly to visit you. You can easily drive to the San Diego airport to pick them up."

♦ American services, merchandise and even jobs are within commuting distance. There's now a Costco Price Club in Tijuana. A border crossing is no longer necessary for that errand! Most cars can be repaired in Mexico, but a specific specialized part is often found in the States.

♦ Business necessities such as cellular phones, pagers and fax machines can be accessed more easily from here. My stateside cellular calls are all made from line of sight to San Diego from a point just south of Tijuana called La Joya. It doesn't work south of that point because it's protected for Mexican cellulars. If I had an analogue, it could be adapted, but costs skyrocket. For a while La Joya point and I will remain frequent friends.

♦ Having a choice about medical help, especially as we grow older, is a priority. A life flight to a major US medical facility is only five minutes. That could make the difference between life and death. However, don't discount Mexican medical expertise. In some cases it's better than anywhere in the world.

♦ Banking can be done in the US. When the peso devalued a few years ago, a lot of people lost money. The option to have money in a stateside account that can be easily accessed is an advantage, especially if you receive checks from the States that need to be cashed. That's not to discount the Mexican banks. Passbook interest of 18-20%

on your money in a Mexican account is a motivating point to consider.

♦ Symphonies, movies, hot dogs and hamburgers are only a half-hour away.

Why are American amenities important while living in a foreign country?

The charm of a foreign culture is to be cherished and appreciated, but being able to choose that which is familiar makes the decision to reside in a foreign country a little easier. Those who choose to live farther south have the challenge of traveling for a day or more to make border runs. The following is an excerpt from my journal:

> While relaxing at the Old Mill Hotel in San Quintin, we met a couple who were traveling south to their home close to Mulege which is an additional ten-hour drive. They had traveled all day from the border in a truck with a huge box made of plywood that enclosed its open bed. Hinges kept the sides together and a little door gave access to the contents inside. We learned that supplies such as toilet paper, nails, food and building supplies from the US filled the box inside to the brim. When the couple said their neighbors had placed orders for desired goods, I pictured the excitement of their return to be much like the Pony Express visiting a remote western village in the 1800s. The box would be dismantled when they arrived home, the truck would be emptied of its precious cargo and the plywood would be used in the construction of their new home. The neighbors would receive their ordered items with warm appreciation. In comparison to their struggles,

our coming and going across the border whenever we wish is much easier. Our lives are much less complicated; but perhaps they'll wean themselves from the US quicker than we will. It's interesting to note that we were on a pleasure trip to San Quintin, while they were on a Pony Express border run.

What is the size of the Rosarito area?

Rosarito encompasses over 20 miles of coastline.

How many people live in the Rosarito area?

According to a census report taken in 1992, there were approximately 100,000 residents.

When did Rosarito become an official municipality of the State of Baja California?

Rosarito changed from a *Delegacion* or suburb of Tijuana to a municipality of the state of Baja California in 1995. It is the newest and fifth municipality in the state. There is a keen sense of city pride among the residents.

What historical sites can I visit in Rosarito Municipality?

♦ At K-53 just east of the Cantamar exit, the site of **Misión Descanso** can be viewed. Take the Descanso exit off the free road to see a chapel that stands on the original site of one of the last Dominican missions, built in 1814.

- The preserved ruins of **San Miguel Arcángel de la Frontera**, the Dominican mission established in 1787, are located at K-65.5 next to the primary school just before the free road curves inland through the hills. The mission was constructed with adobe bricks, some of which are still standing.

- **Calafia**, located on the cliffs above the Pacific with a stunning view, is an historical spot and also a popular restaurant and hotel. Some ruins remain.

- **Museo Wa-Kuatay** is a museum located in downtown Rosarito, north of the Rosarito Beach Hotel. It contains good historical photographs and artifacts concerning the Kumiai Indians, missions and great ranches of Rosarito. Open between 10 AM- 4 PM Wednesday-Monday, there is no admission charge.

- **Rosarito Beach Hotel** is located at the south end of town. Look for the arch. This hotel was a popular get-away spot for the rich in the 1920s. It was famous for gambling and drinking during Prohibition and remains a popular beachfront hotel. Its unique decor includes wall murals and ceiling art that make it a valuable site to visit.

Why is Rosarito Beach Municipality considered the "Jewel of Baja California's Pacific Coast"?

The following are reasons listed on a pamphlet written by the Baja California Secretary of Tourism:

- twenty miles of coastline
- thirty minutes from San Diego
- white sandy beaches

- powerful surf and quiet bays
- magnificent cliff-top views
- rugged mountains and peaceful green valleys
- soaring sand dunes and tranquil tide pools
- year round outdoor paradise
- perfect climate—not too hot, not too cold—naturally air conditioned breeze
- friendly, helpful people
- activities ranging from swimming, surfing, sailing, fishing, golfing, hiking, biking, beachcombing, bogey boarding, horseback riding and relaxing
- colorful sunsets and sunrises
- whale or bird watching
- gourmet dining
- cultural entertainment
- wine festivals
- shopping—bargains for leather, furniture, pottery or folk art
- rest and relaxation

What are some of Ensenada's attractions?

- located seventy miles south of international border
- natural sea geyser—**La Buforada** spouts 60' of ocean water
- cruise ship port

- **Carnaval**—closest Latin Mardi Gras to the United States
- seaside golf
- largest commercial fishing industry
- deep sea fishing
- Hussong's cantina—original building from the 1800s
- winery tours and tastings
- historic **Riviera del Pacifico** convention center—former gambling casino from the 1930s
- Russian settlers
- **Todos Santos Island** and **Todos Santos Bay** marine life
- sea kayaking
- warm Mediterranean climate
- handpainted statue of **Tara**—symbol of Mother Nature overlooking the city
- **Ventana al Mar Park** with gigantic Mexican flying flag
- large seafood market—fresh catches of shrimp, tuna, yellow fish, etc.
- symphonies
- museums

What is noteworthy for the visitor to Tijuana?

- open doors for tourists
- twenty-five minutes from San Diego
- North America's most visited city

- world's most shopped street
- *Jai alai,* world's fastest game
- gourmet restaurants
- hot sulfur springs spa
- convention capital
- international airport
- Omnimax theater
- greyhound racing
- day trips from southern California
- bustling cosmopolitan urban center
- two bullfight rings
- free trade zone
- wax museum
- vibrant nightlife

What is the correct pronunciation of the word Tijuana?

It is pronounced Tee-HWAH-nuh, without the extra "uh" after "tee" that so many people want to put into it. Some think the name came from a ranch called Tia Juana that was destroyed over one hundred years ago, but that is not the correct pronunciation. Please call it Tee-HWAH-nuh and you'll get along well with those who live and work there.

What is the climate of Northern Baja California?

This area has the best weather in all of Central and North America. The climate in Northern Baja California is much the same as that in San Diego. The sun can be shining, the skies blue, but there's a cooling ocean breeze which provides natural air conditioning. The winter temperature varies between 60°-75°F with some rainfall and fog, while the summer temperature has a high of 85°F. A light sweater for the cooling evening temperatures is a must. Be aware that the breeze can lead you to believe that the sun is not tanning your body as rapidly as it is. Inland and southern Baja California have much higher temperature ranges in the summer. Watch the weather channel on television to verify that the weather on the Pacific coast of Northern Baja California is the best in the world. While other areas are having rain or snow, hurricanes or tornadoes, this area is comfortably mild. Rain, wind and high waves will visit for a few days in the winter, reminding us of how lucky we are to have the sun as often as we do. Within a day or two the storm usually blows away leaving behind clear sunny days, fresh air and watered plants.

What are the Santa Ana winds?

These winds generate from the inland deserts, sweep off the mountains and come toward the coastline for a few days in the late summer or early fall. During these days, strange bugs may appear which can be quickly taken care of with bug spray. Dust may fill the air and waves may be high. Don't worry; the winds disappear as quickly as they come. Generally winds go the other way, from the ocean to the mountains, and we don't have adverse effects.

Did *El Niño* cause damage?

El Niño brought high waves and a lot of rain, both of which caused damage during the *El Niño* winter. Poor drainage systems off the hills caused flash floods, and the waves destroyed some docks and a few homes. Insurance companies paid to fix the damage for the lucky ones who had it, and the government repaired the roads as quickly as possible. The following is an excerpt from my journal:

> I enjoyed watching the high waves beat mercilessly upon the shore while the wind and rain washed the rooftops. As long as I was curled up within the walls of my warm home, it was a fascinating phenomenon. Although it bothers me that disasters occurred such as pushing the pink house on the next beach off its foundation, I prefer to look at the blessings that *El Niño* has left behind rather than to dwell upon its destruction. After repairs, our fishing deck, which was torn into little pieces of wood, is now fixed. Instead of being made of wooden planks, it now is made of cement and rocks. It's solidly built for another attack. *El Niño* left an additional unexpected surprise. Our beach, which was so rocky no one dared to walk on it, is now sandy, making it quite useable. There are no more ugly, jagged black rocks in sight. *El Niño* took them away, replacing them with fine white sand. No one can explain it but *El Niño* made it possible for us to use our beach. It was a gift of nature among so much negative destruction.

Is the scenery beautiful in
Northern Baja California?

Wake up in the morning to a different colorful sunrise each day. As the sun sets experience the thrill of the green flash on the horizon as the sun disappears. Then, when the moon comes out, let your eyes be dazzled as the moon shimmers in a pathway across the Pacific. It's truly a place to see nature's paintbrush in action.

Spring brings green hills dotted with wildflowers. Travel into the mountains to see an incredible display of natural beauty similar to the Swiss Alps. I wrote in my journal:

> I couldn't believe I was in Mexico when I first saw the beauty in the hills. I stood on the top of a peak to view the ocean on one side, a flowing river on another and the lush greenery of trees and flowers everywhere. The green hills formed a valley below. Little houses in the distance reminded me of scenes from the movie *The Sound of Music*. I wanted to break into the song, "The Hills Are Alive With The Sound of Music," but alas, I can't carry a tune.

Beach scenes also offer delightful entertainment.

My journal states:

> Yesterday we saw a school of dolphins playfully arching out of the water as they traveled northward in the ocean. It was a breathtaking ballet of graceful movement performed by nature's most delightful creatures. They travel south in the mornings and north in the late afternoons.

Another journal excerpt reads:

> My husband and I have our own binoculars. He likes to watch the girls in bikinis, while I watch the surfers ride the waves. This is a haven for those who love to watch whatever the waves may bring.

Are sunrises lovely in Northern Baja California, Mexico?

Yes. The following description was written while I visited a home on 125 acres in the heartland of the agricultural town of San Quintin:

> It's 6 AM, time for the sun to push itself above the distant hills creating a phenomenon we call morning. Thin stratas of fog hang like terraced ribbons of gossamer along the base of the ring of hills, which rise into the sky as dark, jagged, silhouetted sentinels. Clouds streak the sky above like churning swirls of frosting, floating, vibrant streaks of pink, darker where the sun slowly shows its bright face, lighter and mixed with gray farther away. All nature is churning with delight as the sun at first peeks above the hills and then stretches itself out in its full glorious light. Neighboring roosters take turns echoing each other as they crow to greet the morning light. Birds sing happily and dog barks sleepily while the homes of man lie in quiet stillness. When the sun breaks into full force lighting up the entire atmosphere, the ever-changing mists at length focus into the stability of clear morning air. The vibrant swirling pink clouds have turned to a colorless gray. No longer does time magically hover between night

and morning. The sun has risen and another day has begun in Baja California, Mexico.

What is a *green flash?*

The following is a quote from my friend Peter Rosario:

> Iris and I will sit in front of the big picture windows in our living room to watch the sun set. The horizon on the water is so close to us, we have the illusion that we can just stretch our arms out to touch it. On a clear day when there are no clouds, just at the last instant before the sun disappears, there is a quick flash of green that can be missed in a blink of the eye. This green is a shade that I can't begin to describe. The sun goes down slowly, seeming not to even move, but it disappears bit by bit. Then, just as it totally drops below the horizon, the last sliver of color flashes green, not red. We've been able to catch it a few times but it's illusive. Witnessing Mother Nature's paint brush at work is one of the pleasures of living on the water's edge.

Another friend, Kathy Wasson says:

> While watching the sun go down, I've seen the green flash several times. Just as the water swallows up the sun, a vibrant neon green line is cast along the water's edge. It's absolutely beautiful but it disappears as quickly as it comes.

Steve Edwards, a staff writer for the *Muskegon Michigan Chronicle*, describes it as follows:

If conditions are right, a burst of emerald light occurs at the last moment of sunset or just as the sun breaks the horizon at sunrise. As the sun dips below the horizon, its rays are split into a rainbow-like spectrum of light—red at the bottom, blue on top and green in the middle. The blue is almost impossible to see, but the green appears for an instant and then is gone. Baja's unpolluted surroundings make it a perfect place to see a green flash.

Lastly, Adolfo Kim says:

Seeing the green flash means you'll have good luck. God is very good to us. He gives us the sunrise and the sunset to keep us happy. When we see the green flash, he is smiling down upon us. We're so lucky to be able to feel and see His love for us.

Why does the sea look phosphorescent?

A summer sea between the months of May to October may have a phosphorescent glow due to the warming of the water, which causes a plant called *Gonyanlux* to grow underwater. This plant is very poisonous. It contaminates the shellfish in the area causing them to be dangerously poisonous to eat. Don't eat the shellfish from those waters. Just enjoy the shimmering beauty of the ocean.

Why do people choose to live in Baja California, Mexico?

The following are direct quotes from those who have chosen to live in the Rosarito area:

From the first time I set foot in Mexico, I knew this is where I would someday live. I came here from back east with no expectations. My mind and heart were open and I came away with so much more than I ever dreamed possible. This first trip was approximately eighteen years ago. Intrigued by the raw beauty of the countryside and the pure power and magnificence of the ocean, I came back to visit year after year until six years ago. I decided enough was enough. I gave notice to my employer, sold my house, kissed my lovely grown children good-bye and moved 3000 miles away to Baja California, Mexico. I have never regretted this move for even a moment. I wasn't running away from anything but I was running to my destiny. A spiritual strength of peace and power radiates from the ocean. It first drew me here and now it sustains me day after day, leaving me always in awe. I live on less than a thousand dollars a month, but I have it all. I own a lovely home with a view of the ocean on one side and hills and mountains on the other. It's a place to die for. I love the Mexican people. They know how to experience life in the NOW. They understand that yesterday is gone, and that tomorrow isn't here yet. Today is a gift. The now is all anyone has. They enjoy it moment by moment before it slips into yesterday and is lost forever. They live the reality of this universal truth. So do I. I know I belong here with them. I tell people that my nationality is *gringa* but my *corazon* (heart) is *Mexicana*. Mexico is where I choose to live and die. I will never go back to live in the United States. This is my home.

—Kathy Wasson,
San Antonio Del Mar,
Baja California, Mexico

C H A P T E R   T H R E E
BORDER CROSSING

The moment your car clears the gate and
enters that befuddling montage of alien signs,
mad traffic, and pitted streets, you know that you
are no longer under the benign protection of the
U.S. flag. You are in Mexico, a very foreign land.

—Jack Smith
God and Mr. Gomez

Is it possible to rent a car for travel across the border into Mexico?

Yes. Not all rental agencies allow cars to cross the border, but there are some companies that will rent if full Mexican coverage is purchased from them. Be certain to compare prices of the insurance as well as the rental costs. Proof of insurance and the rental agreement should be in the car at all times. Make a copy to be kept elsewhere in case the car is stolen. When you go back across the border, the US customs officer may ask if you own the car. When you say no it will trigger a trunk search. Be ready to show the rental agreement.

The following companies rent cars for travel in Mexico:

+ **Bob Baker Ford Rental**—(619) 297-3106. Free pickup service is offered. Everything from luxury cars to 4x4s to 15-person vans are available to take across the border. Non-smoking cars are available.

+ **California Baja, Rent-A-Car**—1-888-470-RENT or (619) 470-2004. This company allows cars to travel the full length of Baja. They provide airport pickup but a charge is added to your bill. All styles of cars and vans are available including RVs and motor homes. Webpage address: http://www.cabaja.com

+ **Budget Rent A Car**—This national chain offers rental cars for Mexican travel on two conditions. Mexican insurance must be purchased through them at the rate of $20 a day in addition to the rental charge. Cars can't travel any further south than Ensenada.

What should I expect when crossing the border into Mexico?

Going south into Mexico is a lot easier than the return to the States because the wait isn't as long. Plan to go through before or after commute time because there are many who travel across the border to work in San Diego, making the lines of cars long between four and six o'clock for the return south to Mexico. If you're legally bringing in items for sale or moving a houseful of furniture, there's a lane for Declared items (see page 317 for information about moving). A receipt showing the value of the items could save time and confusion as the Mexican official computes the tariff. The amount will be reasonable compared to what would happen if you get caught trying to get goods across illegally.

As you pass over the border, your car will trigger either a green or red light. Some say every 13th car gets the red light. Others say the weight of the car triggers the red light. It's like the lottery. Most of the time you'll get a green *pase* or pass light and can move ahead without stopping. If you don't get a green light, it will be a red light saying *alto*, which means stop. Pull into the search lane and stop. An inspector will ask you questions such as, "Where are you going?" or "What are you bringing into Mexico?" Just answer the questions honestly and don't chat. Offering too much information is not necessary. The Mexican customs official may just poke at your luggage or he may do a full search, opening your entire luggage and looking primarily for weapons, drugs or electronic equipment. If nothing is suspicious, you'll be allowed to go ahead.

Be aware that there are many stories told about people who are caught with electronic equipment in their car. Their cars are impounded until high fines are paid and they are bodily taken back into the States in a quick deportation. To carry guns is a felony, so jail is the fate of those who get caught with them. I came very close to having an unpleasant experience without knowing it.

On a day when I had placed my laptop computer, which was in a black leather briefcase, in the trunk of my car in order to get it programmed for the Mexican Internet provider in Tijuana, I ended up crossing the border to the US for a quick errand. On my return south to Mexico, I got the *alto* or stop signal. I pulled over for inspection. The official asked me why I was coming into Mexico. I replied that I lived in Rosarito. I hadn't recalled that my computer was in the trunk until the Mexican customs official told me to open it for inspection. There the computer sat, with nothing around it. He obviously saw the black briefcase. It was on the tip of my tongue to say, "Oh, it's my personal computer." I had no knowledge that carrying it across the border without declaring it was a serious offense. Thank goodness I never got the words out before he closed the trunk. He didn't know it was a computer because he didn't open the briefcase. I guess I was an unwitting smuggler. I was a lucky, unwitting smuggler.

Another time I discovered how commuters get to the front of the line when there's congestion. They simply take the last San Ysidro exit off the freeway. The off ramp parallels the freeway for about a half-mile. Before the car reaches the intersecting road, it simply goes over the divider between the off ramp and the freeway, thus returning to the freeway. When another car lets it into the congested lane, a half-mile of waiting has been avoided. Valuable time has been saved successfully, if not legally.

One time while waiting in line to enter into Mexico we saw a man running across the US border away from pursuing Mexican officials toward the US. Once across he looked backwards to see if he was still being chased. He slowed down when he realized he was safely across the border away from his Mexican pursuers who ventured no farther than the invisible border line. He was elated to have escaped being caught by them, but I wondered what would happen when the US custom officials confronted him. I also wondered what he had done in Mexico. I guess I'll never know, but I do know this—I never want that to happen to me. I'd probably trip before getting across the border safely and I'd end up being hauled off to a Mexican jail.

While waiting in a line of cars to go across the border into Mexico during commuting time, I heard a symphony of horn honking, one after another, just after one car blasted his horn. It was as though this one car woke everyone up to the fact that there was congestion ahead. It seemed that not one of the hundreds of cars waiting to go through the border wanted to be left out of delivering the message to move ahead. Since then I've learned that honking horns are common sounds in Mexican cities.

Don, a neighbor at Club Marena, related the following incident:

> I went into the "declaration" lane when I brought a sofa across the border into Mexico with a receipt showing what I paid for it. I told the official I was getting it re-upholstered in Rosarito. He said, "I'll make you a deal. You push the button. If it's green you'll get to take it across free but if it's red, you'll have to pay the tariff." I pushed the button. It was green, so I went across the border without having to pay.

Others say:

> There are scales imbedded in the roadway at the border

crossing. If you keep your right tires on the pavement as you go through the Mexican border, you'll always get the green light because the red light is triggered by the weight of your car.

If you keep the front of your car right up against the back fender of the car ahead, you can pass through on the other car's *pase* or green light.

Are there any controls over the underage youth who attempt to come into Mexico to party from the United States side of the border?

Yes. The law enforcement agencies station themselves at the border to prevent partying minors from going into Mexico during holiday weekends. They will detain them, determine their age and then will call parents to take them home. Four thousand were turned back during the 1998 New Year's weekend. If a minor returns to the States inebriated, he should expect to be greeted by United States law enforcement officials who will handle him accordingly.

Are there any controls over cars leaving the United States at the border?

Recently the United States placed several cement lane dividers to slow traffic as it approaches the border at San Ysidro. A camera takes pictures of license plates before the cars cross over into Mexico. Several criminals have been prevented from leaving the country in this manner.

What dangers do we face when crossing into Mexico?

US citizens get into trouble when they get to an overpass near Tejas where I-10 and US 54 converge. They accidentally get onto an international bridge and can't get off without going through the Mexican border. If they have a gun in the car they're thrown into jail indefinitely because possession of a gun is a felony with a five-30-year jail sentence attached. United States authorities would like the Mexican authorities to discern between "accidents" and intent to get arms into Mexico.

> OHIO SENIOR FREED FROM MEXICAN JAIL, the Associated Press, Lebanon, Ohio—An Ohio man who said he accidentally entered Mexico last week with a rifle in his pickup truck was released Thursday, much to the joy of his family in this southwest Ohio city. Ed Hollingsworth said he made a wrong turn last Thursday in Douglas, Arizona, and wound up at a Mexican border checkpoint. Mexican authorities spotted the .22-caliber rifle in his truck and arrested him on a charge he was trying to smuggle weapons into Mexico, his family was told . . .

What are some of the freedoms I have in Mexico that I don't have in the US ?

♦ No restrictions about smoking exist in bars or restaurants.

♦ Dogs can run freely on the beach.

♦ Campfire and tents are allowed on the beach for overnight camping.

- Drinking at age 18 is allowed.
- Cars don't have to be equipped with smog devices.
- Bull and cockfights are allowed.
- Homes can be built without a lot of restrictions at a reasonable cost.
- Medical procedures may be obtained in Mexico that are not allowed in the US.

What are the phone numbers for US border crossing stations?

San Ysidro - (619) 639-7100

Otay Mesa - (619) 661-3249

Tecate - (619) 478-5545

News Flash: A new border crossing at La Playas in Tijuana is planned for the near future. It will shorten the wait.

Are the borders open all hours?

San Ysidro - Open 24 hours daily

Otay Mesa - Open daily 6 AM to 10 PM

Tecate - Open daily 6 AM to midnight

What is the San Ysidro Tourist Information phone number and address?

(619) 428-6200

4570 Camino de la Plaza, San Ysidro, CA 92173

How do I get to Tijuana, Rosarito or Ensenada after crossing the San Ysidro border?

The roads are clearly marked with signs to Tijuana reading *El Centro* or to the toll road or *Cuota* heading south reading **Rosarito-Ensenada Scenic Route**, or **Rosarito-Ensenada Cuota**. You'll see signs to the *Playas* of Tijuana but stay to the left and you'll eventually come to the toll booth. The first or north exit to Rosarito is approximately 18 miles from the San Ysidro border crossing. Continue on the toll road to Ensenada. The road is a paved four-lane highway which will have three toll booths to collect under $2.00 (depending upon the rate of exchange) from you each time you reach a booth.

Is local bus service available?

Yes. The local Mexican bus is easily available across the street from the Rosarito Beach Hotel. It leaves every 20 minutes from 6 AM to 9 PM daily and charges $1.00 for travel to Tijuana. It also provides service south to Ensenada.

Where is the bus station located in Tijuana?

There are two locations in Tijuana, the old downtown terminal at Calle Comercio and Avenida Madero, and the new Central Bus Terminal serving eastern Tijuana on Boulevard Lazaro Cardenas at Boulevard Alamar. Phone: (011) (52) 66-86-9515 for more information.

Are the buses comfortable?

Yes. They are generally clean and comfortable, but remember that they are not tour buses. The bus drivers may or may not speak English.

Is there a shuttle service to and from Rosarito and the border?

There is a shuttle bus to and from the border, which picks up and delivers directly to the Rosarito Hotel. The cost is approximately $15 per adult, while up to two children less than 12 years old are free. Reservations are necessary in advance with a 24-hour cancellation notice required. Phone: (011-52) (661) 2-01-44.

To be picked up at the border, go to the waiting room located within the tourism office building just 50 feet from the second steel rotary gate. Parking is available for cars to be left at the border.

Are taxis available in Rosarito?

Yes. Cabs are lined up for business at the south end of town. Be aware that the rate of charge should be indicated somewhere inside the taxicab. Be certain to negotiate the charge before entering the cab and ask to see the rate chart before accepting the offered price.

The local Mexican residents use taxicabs much like a bus for local transportation. The cabs will stop along the way to pick up those who are waiting. If you want the cab to be private, you will pay accordingly.

In order to catch a cab in Tijuana that will go to Rosarito for a reasonable charge, go to Madero Street and find a cab that says Rosarito Beach on it. State whether or not you want private service and negotiate the cost up front.

Unlike the problems in Mexico City, there is no concern in Northern Baja California with cab drivers attacking tourists. Quite the contrary. The cab drivers are very helpful and courteous.

Is it possible to travel on a bus from Los Angeles or San Diego to Tijuana?

Yes. Check with the Greyhound bus service in each city for the fare and time schedules. Make certain to identify the location of the arrival terminal, so there is no confusion upon arrival in Tijuana. Call (800) 231-2222.

Is it possible to travel by bus from Tijuana to La Paz?

Yes. There are two different services available, **Autotrasportes de Baja California** or (**ABC**) and **Tres Estrellas de Oro**. Phone: (011) (52) 66-26-170.

The trip takes about 24 hours with two different drivers. One sleeps in the luggage compartment while the other drives.

Is a shuttle service available from the border to Tijuana?

Yes. Leaving every half-hour, **Mexicoach** is very clean and comfortable. Look for the bright red bus at the pay parking lots on the US side of the border. You'll be dropped off at the Tijuana Tourist Terminal in the heart of downtown on *Revolution* between 7th and 8th Street. Call (619) 428-9517.

Is it possible to walk across the border?

Yes. Park your car in any pay parking lot in the US and simply walk across the border. Taxi cabs and buses are available once you get across. Expect a bag search.

Is it possible to take the San Diego trolley to the border?

Yes. This is one way to travel to and from San Diego without waiting in long lines to cross over the border. Trolley times are regular and the cost is minimal. Many commuters find this way of travel to be the answer to commuting problems. Call (619) 231-8549 for more information.

What advice do you have for those who live in Mexico and have to cross the border into the United States?

If you plan to live in Mexico, you should rid yourself of expectations in order to just experience each day with all the activities or adventures it brings. Do not allow judgmental thoughts such as "If they would only do it this way . . ." or "I have the answer for these people . . . " It's easy to slip into negative thinking. For instance, one day when I was planning to cross the border, I was diverted into downtown Tijuana because the main road was flooded. As I traveled along the detour, a parade of every police car and ambulance in the city was taking place downtown, right on my route to the border. Not a car was able to move. I found myself thinking, "It just doesn't make sense to block the entire traffic flow just to parade the city vehicles . . ." then I told myself to just laugh, because it makes perfect sense to them . . . in some way. Just because I can't figure out what it is doesn't matter. Adolfo Kim's words from a past incident floated through my mind saying, "Roberta, relax. There's nothing to worry about. You're in my country. Remember, you're in Mexico now . . ." Mentally I replied, "OK. I'll just chuckle at myself while I wait. So what if I'm late. I live in Mexico now!"

Going north out of Mexico, which exit do I take off the Cuota or toll road to return to the San Ysidro border?

A couple of miles after passing through the final tollbooth look for the green signs that read **San Diego-Tecate**. Follow the signs to the right, not the one that says **Centro**. After the turn, immediately move over to the far-left lane to take the first turn left. Signs on the left side of the road will say **San Ysidro Border**. Turn left and follow the signs that read **San Diego-Rio Zone**. The border fence will be on your far left. Follow this road until you have to turn. Get over to the right lane as soon as you make the left. You will immediately go right onto a ramp that is labeled

San Diego. Get into the middle lane and prepare to wait in lines at the border.

Is there a way to get through the US border quickly?

Yes. It costs $129 per year. There is a dedicated commuter lane at Otay Mesa, which prevents a long wait at the border. Open hours are from 6 AM to 8 PM M-F, and 8 AM to 6 PM on weekends. Those who live in Northwest Baja California can easily access this border, located within 15 minutes of the San Ysidro border. If you need to cross the border often, consider spending the extra money. The time saved not waiting in line makes it worthwhile. If you have a criminal record, forget it. You will never get a pass. The exciting news is that by the time this book is published a commuter's lane will be open at the San Ysidro border as well. The processing will take between four to six weeks. Call (619) 661-3171 for information. There should be no more waiting in line for hours to cross the border into the United States!

Another way to get through the San Ysidro border quickly is to know which lanes to access. You must learn how to avoid the *Gringo* lines, which are to the far left. The locals use the lanes to the right behind the stalls because they are usually shorter. In order to access these lanes, take the lane to the right behind the stalls as you approach the border. It is labeled **for carpools** with white diamonds painted on the pavement. If you have three or more passengers in your car, you may stay in that lane. If you have less than three passengers, you must move to a lane to the right. Someone will let you in front of them if you ask politely.

What are license plate scanners?

They are computerized scanners used at the San Ysidro border by the US customs to recognize the activity of a vehicle at border crossings. When a car pulls up to the customs booth, a picture of the license plate is put through a scanner which can access information about any outstanding arrest warrants, stolen vehicle reports or any other incidentals concerning that particular license plate number. Cars that have carried contraband goods in the past will be red-flagged by the scanner. They're suspect and will immediately be searched. In this way, criminals can be caught and suspicious activity curtailed. The following is an example.

A woman was stopped for a car search because the license scanner indicated that on a previous crossing her car had contained goods that required import duties. In this search prompted by the scanner, a human skull was found on the back seat in a plastic bag. She was detained for questioning. She said she purchased the skull from a "medicine woman" in Tijuana. Without the use of the scanner, she may not have been stopped.

These scanners not only help catch criminals at the border, but they speed up time spent waiting to cross, because the innocent who don't require a search can pass through quickly.

The following are words from an FBI agent:

> The system they use at all the borders, international airports and other ports of entry into the United States is called Techs, which is sponsored by US Customs. This system keeps track of all the vehicle license plates,

passports, visas, etc. that are moving across international boundaries entering the United States. It has the capability of placing look-outs to flag suspected violators for customs violations. Names of most suspected smugglers are placed in the system, which may alert the Customs Inspector to check out the person or vehicle more carefully. Agencies such as the FBI, US Marshal or other law enforcement agencies can place look-outs on violators and can even place notification parameters upon entry of the suspects.

A good example is if I know that a person is traveling to a foreign country and I want to know where he/she goes and with whom he/she meets outside the United States, I can place a look-out on that individual returning from abroad. I once found a fugitive in jail in Cuba by placing a look-out on his wife. When she went to visit her husband in jail in Cuba she returned with his inmate number and institution address. If Cuba had an extradition agreement with the United States, he would be in custody. At least I know where he is right now. As you can imagine, the number of people and vehicles passing through the ports of entry each day is voluminous. The inspectors don't have to harass the normal everyday citizen. They try to use the computers to assist them in locating patterns and suspects involved in smuggling. The best tool is still an experienced inspector with good instincts and a keen eye.

What do the signs above the border stations say in both Spanish and English?

♦ Report smuggling—call 1-800 BE ALERT.

- You may be inspected while waiting in line.
- Don't disturb the dogs; they are working. Don't whistle.
- Failure to declare items could result in loss of items and a fine.
- Don't bring more than $10,000 across the border.
- Declare agricultural products even if purchased in the United States.

What questions will I be asked at the US border?

- Where is your place of birth?
- How long were you in Mexico?
- Are you the owner of this car?
- What items are you bringing with you?
- Could I see your driver's license?
- Would you unlock your trunk from the inside, please? No, don't get out.

How do I answer the US border guard's questions?

Tips for answering:

- Don't joke around with these border guards. They're trained to be quite serious and they could cost you a lot of time if they choose.
- Be honest and truthful.

- You may be asked to show your driver's license or vehicle registration.

- Each person in the car may be asked to speak, so don't try to answer for everyone.

- Say, "Howdy" for a greeting. They'll immediately recognize you as a US citizen.

What should I expect when crossing the border into the US going north?

Going north to the states is entirely more time consuming if you're not aware of these hints:

- Dogs may sniff at your car, so don't get nervous.

- Don't try to hide illegal persons, drugs, weapons or goods.

- Don't talk on a cellular phone as you approach the customs station.

- You may legally return with up to $400 worth of personal goods per person, and one liter of liquor, wine or beer in addition to 100 cigars (not Cuban) and 200 cigarettes (if you're over 21 years of age). Food items and plants are restricted as well.

- Call for the wait time at 01-66-83-14-05 or listen to the San Diego radio stations' border reports on the news.

- There are weekday car pool lanes for three or more persons per car between 5 AM and 10 PM at the San Ysidro border.

- Best time to cross is between 8:45 AM and 9:30 AM on

week days—more lanes are open to accommodate commuters who have already gone through the border.

♦ The Otay Mesa border crossing is open between 6 AM and 10 PM and may be a way to avoid weekend or holi day traffic. It also issues yearly commuter passes for a small fee. To find this border crossing, follow the airport signs northeast of Tijuana heading toward Mexicali. Watch for **Garita de Otay** signs and follow them until you cross on Highway 905, which will later connect with I-805 and I-5.

Waiting to cross the border into the United States can be tedious. However, the following experiences illustrate that humor can lighten the wait.

"I'm not going to buy another Mexican item," my friend Carol announced as we approached the lines of cars at the border. She saw the man with the blankets on his back going from car to car offering "the best prices" for his wares and was determined to resist his advances. Our car was already bulging with bags of goodies purchased during our "shop 'til you drop" weekend women's get-away. Carol resisted the blankets, but when the spotted cow piggy bank came around, it somehow ended up in our car as an intended gift to her husband. We roared with laughter as we each bought more trinkets from these "last minute" peddlers. Little hand-blown glass hummingbirds that would make good Christmas tree ornaments proved to be my weakness, while an Aztec calendar was squeezed into the car for Gayle, the third member of our party. She, the owner of the car, lived in California, allowing her to take home the large, bulky items that Carol and I had to avoid because we couldn't carry them on our flight home-ward to Oregon. When we were asked by the US customs official if we had purchased anything, we roared with laughter and said we didn't leave much in Mexico. He laughed with us and let us leave without further inspection.

On another occasion, I had to go to the bathroom so badly when I waited in a particularly slow line. I was so desperate to solve my problem I finally yielded to using an empty plastic drink cup that was luckily on the floor beside me. I hunkered down as far as I could so no one would see me, filled the cup, and replaced the lid. From now on I make certain I carry a larger container with me. I came very close to overflow. How embarrassing!

Here's an anecdote told by Pam Garcia of Rosarito:

> Another tense moment while waiting in the line at the border going north into the United States occurred when the narc dog who sniffs out drugs stopped at my car. I remember thinking, "Oh, my gosh, here I am, a woman who is a grandmother, who has never done anything illegal in her life, and I'm going to get caught because someone planted drugs in my car. How would I explain it? Who could have done such a horrible thing to me?" I silently mulled over the names of my acquaintances wondering what I could have done to offend one of them enough to set me up for what would be the most horrible experience of my life. I came up blank. My friends weren't the types to do this. They were mothers or grandmothers too. They wouldn't know what drugs even looked like, let alone set me up for a drug run.
>
> The other thought that raced through my whole body, making me shake with fear, was the underlying

blackness of anticipating spending the remaining years of my life in jail instead of lounging by the beach. What if I'm thrown in the same cell with women who are evil? How could I cope? Those thoughts seemed to take more than the seconds that passed by as the dog sniffed my tire, then lifted his leg to do his business. He must have sniffed the tire, found another dog's scent and decided to make his mark too. He wasn't sniffing narcotics on my car. Hooray! I was off the hook! My friends aren't drug runners after all. I get to live my life as planned.

Waiting to go through the border can be a very disagreeable waste of time if a person allows it to be. On the other hand, it can be turned into a gift of time. I've decided to set it aside as a special time to get little chores accomplished such as polishing my fingernails, writing little thank you notes, cleaning out my purse or making phone calls on my cellular phone. It takes the pressure off to tell myself, "I'll do that little chore while waiting at the border." Somehow I feel more organized and it's eliminated the negative from the border wait.

Judy Sager reports another border experience:

> When I first moved here I was very nervous about going through the border into the United States. My anticipation grew with each moment I waited in line, which seemed to drag on and on. Even though I had nothing to hide, I didn't know what to expect when I'd finally reach the customs booth. During the wait my anticipation grew when the dogs sniffed my tires. Then I had to fend off other cars that tried to cut in front of me, selfishly speeding up their own wait at my

expense. After approximately 40 minutes, I finally arrived to face the man in the booth. I timidly rolled my window down to answer the dreaded anticipated questions. Looking into my car with suspicion, the man in the uniform asked, "What is your country of origin?" I immediately said, "Bakersfield." The incredulous look he gave me made me even more nervous. He asked, "Bakersfield is your country of origin?" His reaction snapped me out of my senior moment to say, "No. I mean the United States." He cracked a smile turning it shortly into a laugh. I could feel my face turning red but after that first moment of humiliation, I ended up joining him in a hearty chuckle. He motioned me to move on without an inspection. I passed the interrogation and was able to continue on my way. Now I smile every time I think about what a fool I made of myself. I no longer fear going through the border.

C H A P T E R   F O U R

DRIVING IN
BAJA CALIFORNIA

Slow down, my dear; there's more time than life.
—Mama Espinoza
El Rosario

What items shall I bring in my car in order to travel the roads of Baja California?

♦ A **tourist card** if you're traveling south of Ensenada or staying for more than 72 hours. Get it stamped at the port of entry or at the *Migracion* or immigration office in Ensenada. The tourist card can be obtained from the Mexican consulate closest to your home town. In order to get it, you'll need your passport, birth certificate or voter registration card in order to prove your citizenship. If one parent is traveling with a minor (under 18), written permission from the other is needed, and if a minor is alone, written proof of permission from both parents is necessary. There is no need to carry a passport if you have a tourist card.

♦ **Valid driver's license** from your home state as well as the original registration for the vehicle in your possession.

♦ **Good tires, a can of "fix a flat"** sealer and a good spare because the roads can have *vados*, dips, or *topes*, speed bumps, as well as streets made of little round stones. San Antonio Del Mar, a neighborhood just north of Rosarito on the ocean, has all three of these little tire-challenging obstacles. Dirt roads are common, but main traveling routes are paved. The following incident illustrates another handy way to solve the problem of a flat tire.

When my husband and I took the three-hour trip from Ensenada to San Quintin, our right back tire went flat. We were lucky enough to be driving in tandem with Andrés Meling, who immediately opened his hood to attach an air pump he had installed in his engine to our tire, which was restored to its original condition in just seconds. He then took us to the nearest *llantera*, or tire shop, which fixed our flat for $1.50. How lucky we were in the company of a good friend who is the most valued, seasoned guide in all of Baja California. He had the right solution to the immediate problem! Since then, we've noticed there are tire shops everywhere there's a town. Look for the word, *llantera*, written on a sign or big tire in front of a tire shop. It's odd that we never saw the signs until we had our little flat tire experience in San Quintin.

◆ **Pesos or dollars for toll**—The toll cost varies with the fluctuation of the peso. Currently, it is 16 pesos or $1.60 (value fluctuates). If you use dollars, they may or may not have the correct cents to give you change, so have a supply of pesos for this purpose. Save the toll road receipt. It is your insurance receipt should you have an accident while driving on the *Cuota* or pay road.

◆ **Green Angels**—Radio-dispatched Green trucks help distressed vehicles. There are telephones every mile rotating northbound with southbound. Gasoline, battery cables, etc. are dispatched as needed. (See page 72.)

◆ **Pesos or dollars for gasoline**—Don't expect to use your credit cards, personal checks or traveler's checks in Mexico for gasoline and don't let your tank get really low. On some holiday weekends the demand for gas from tourists causes the gas stations to run out. Magnasin gas is unleaded. PeMex fuel is all you will find. Premium may be the answer if your engine "pings" and lugs up hills. Be certain to watch the figures on the pump and stand around while your tank is being filled. Remember that liters, not gallons, are used for gasoline in Mexico. 1 gallon=3.784 liters.

◆ **Extra cans** of oil, fan belts, window cleaner, toilet paper, and water—cars get very dirty because of the dirt roads, and moist, salty air. Toilet paper and bottled water can be purchased in Mexican stores.

◆ **Security devices**—When a car is parked, "The Club" or an alarm system is recommended. Don't drive at night and don't leave your car unprotected. There is a very effective device that clips onto the steering wheel showing a flashing red light. Pep Boys sells this S.W.A.T. for under $30. An alarm goes off if it is jiggled. I highly recommend installing an "engine kill switch" so that the motor can't be started without a key. When parking, back into the parking spot to make towing your car a little more difficult. As a precaution, never leave anything of value in your car. Don't be paranoid, but do be wise. It is prudent to watch over your possessions.

◆ **Cellular phone**—Either purchase a phone from Baja Cellular or Telcel or convert your phone to Mexican service at Mexican cellular companies which can be found in Rosarito, Tijuana or Ensenada. A new digital phone is now on the market that works in Baja California. Analogues were the only cellulars that operated in Mexico for a while.

◆ **Tools**—Any small tool kit will do, but Sears has a compact toolbox filled with everything from screwdrivers to hammers for no more than $30.

◆ **Medical supplies**—Band-Aids, bug spray, peroxide, aspirin, Tums, Maalox, etc. I just learned of a lightweight portable splint that can be carried easily in a backpack or medical emergency kit. It is capable of immobilizing almost any bone in the body and doesn't have to be removed when taking X-rays. It's pliable enough to fit anyone, yet firm enough to splint any broken bone. It adds no weight and is a fabulous invention. For more information, call 1-800-818-4726. Tell them Roberta recommended it for Baja California activities and trips.

◆ **Bungy cords**, duct tape, vice grips, jumper cables, emergency flares.

◆ **Spanish-English dictionary**—Never know when you'll need it!

◆ **Flashlight**—Be certain the batteries are new.

+ **Pepper spray**—Hang on your belt or keep within easy reach.

+ **List of phone numbers** for American consulate, insurance carrier and legal counsel, Secretary of Tourism for Baja California and emergency phone numbers. (See pages 170, 173, and 209 for telephone numbers.)

+ **Extension cord**—This item would have come in handy for me to have been able to use my curling iron comfortably while staying in a motel room that only had one electrical plug located by the door, too far from a mirror.

+ **Blanket**—The temperature falls at night especially during the winter. You'll be warm if you have your own blanket. Some motels don't offer more than one thin blanket on the bed, especially if you travel south. Consider taking an emergency space blanket for lightweight carrying.

+ **Spray disinfectant**—Cleanliness varies.

+ **Little heater**—In the winter this little item could make a room cozily warm. Beware, some motels run off generators that are turned off at night.

+ **Extra headlights** on the car—Adding large headlights to a vehicle may allow night driving on the trans-peninsular highway where cows or wild animals cause a problem by appearing unexpectedly on the road.

Do I need Mexican car insurance while driving in Mexico?

Yes. Whether your US insurance company covers you south of the border or not, you need Mexican insurance even if it's only liability insurance. If coverage is by a Mexican insurance company, you will be able to prove that you are capable of making payment for damage you may have caused. Because you are considered guilty until proven innocent in Mexico, you could be spending time in jail with your car impounded until the case goes to court unless you have Mexican insurance, which may prevent an unpleasant detention. Some American insurance companies will cover your car up to 50 miles south of the border, but check your policy. If you have this coverage, then purchase only Mexican liability only insurance. If you aren't covered, obtain full comprehensive Mexican insurance. You should ask the insurance company if an adjuster or legal service is offered. You should be provided with a proof of insurance card to carry in your wallet. It will have the names of whom to call for help if you are detained. Remember you're in a foreign country. It is not the same as in the US. The Mexican government does not consider any other country's policies valid in Mexico. You need to follow the accepted procedure of the country.

What is liability only insurance?

It is the minimum insurance required by Mexican law. It covers payment for damage caused by your automobile, including death and injury to another party, and medical coverage for persons riding in your car. You, as a driver of any vehicle, may purchase it, or it can be included in full comprehensive coverage on a specific car.

What questions do I consider when shopping for car insurance?

Ask these questions:

+ What is the coverage?
+ Will it cover a trailer/boat I will be pulling?
+ What is the deductible?
+ Is legal aid included?
+ What is the cost?
+ How long will I be covered?
+ Who is covered? Anyone who drives the car?
+ Is the parent company a Mexican company? If not, it may not be considered legal in Mexico.
+ How quickly will I get help from the insurance company?

Note: Call the Mexican parent company to verify that the agent has sent in your paperwork. Some people have found they are not covered because the agent pocketed the money.

Note: If a Mexican insurance company claims to cover you in the United States, beware. The United States may not consider the insurance valid and you could be cited for driving without insurance.

Where do I purchase Mexican automobile insurance?

It is advisable to shop around. There are many sources and prices available:

♦ Clubs such as **AAA**, **Vagabundos Del Mar** or **Sanborn's Mexico Club** have group rates that you can purchase from the states.

♦ Internet sites such as **bajaquest.com** or **bajasun.com** allow you to purchase Mexican insurance from the com fort of your home.

♦ US border towns have many signs guiding you to a company that may be open 24 hours a day.

♦ Tijuana and Rosarito have many insurance companies to serve you. **Bernie's Mexican Insurance** (011-52-6) 612-1028 or **The Baja Insurance Services** (011-52-661) 2-14-44 have lower prices. If you're planning a long stay, you may want to check their offerings. You could obtain temporary coverage at the border until you arrange more permanent and less expensive coverage locally.

Shop around. It may save you a lot of money. Remember, don't travel without Mexican automobile insurance.

How do I import my vehicle into Mexico?

Since there are no permit requirements in Baja California or Baja California del Sur, most people just bring their vehicles across the border, maintaining licensing in the States. If the car is taken to the mainland by ferry, it will need a permit in order to cross. On the peninsula the license plate should be updated yearly with current stickers in order to keep the Mexican police from stopping the vehicle. Some states will allow the renewal process to be completed by mail, while others require the car to pass local emissions testing, causing the car to be returned each year for testing. If a car is purchased in Mexico, expect to pay 3.5% tax on the purchase price as well as registration fees. AAA, the Mexican consulate closest to your hometown and the Mexican government offices in Mexico will have the necessary forms and will assist in this process of registering a vehicle that will cross into the mainland of Mexico. The AAA office in Chula Vista is located at 569 Telegraph Canyon Rd., Chula Vista, California 92010. Call (619) 421-0410 for more information.

How do I obtain a Mexican driver's license?

Obtaining a Mexican driver's license is an easy process if you have a current valid license from the United States or Canada. Go to local license office in the town in which you live. You don't have to take a test, but you will be asked for the following:

♦ Copy of current driver's license—you should have original with you to show; they won't take it away.

♦ Passport-size front view picture of you.

♦ Copy of your legal paperwork such as the FM-3 — plan to show original.

♦ Copy of utility bill with name and address on it.

♦ Cost is currently 77 pesos. It will fluctuate and change.

Possessing a Mexican driver's license will give you added

respect from the police if you are stopped for traffic violations.

What permits or licenses are required for travel in Baja California?

* Valid U.S. or Canadian driver's licenses are honored in all of Mexico.

* Car permits are not required in any part of the Baja peninsula. However, they are required if a ferry is taken to the mainland. If you plan to travel to the mainland, obtain a car permit at the border when you first cross over to Mexico.

* Carry an original vehicle registration from your home state at all times.

* If you don't own the vehicle, carry a letter of permission from the owner.

* Carry your tourist visa or other legal documentation of your right to be in the country. If you're leaving Northern Baja California, Mexico, within 72 hours, you don't need it.

* Don't drive a car with a Mexican license plate unless you have a Mexican driver's license. It's against the law.

* Don't let a Mexican national drive your car. It's illegal.

What hints do you have for driving?

* Be on the alert for **stop** signs which read *alto* located on the right or left sides of the main street where there are

intersecting off roads. These signs are easy to miss not only because the location is off to the side, but because they may sometimes be very faded or missing altogether. Hint: Watch the flow of the traffic around you and stop when others do.

- Drivers will turn left in a U-turn at a stop sign. The oncoming traffic that also has a stop sign will be patient while it is done. It won't be long before you too will be doing it but until you get accustomed to the habit, it could take you by surprise. Be alert as you go forward from a stop.

- Be aware that some of the side streets off the main road are one way. These signs show up when least expected. The signs are very small and are easy to miss because they're located in an obscure place. One of the one-way streets in Rosarito goes right past the police station. You definitely don't want to make a mistake because ignorance won't pay the fine.

- The far right lane is not a driving lane. It is a lane for bicycles and for taxis to stop for passengers. It also makes backing out of parking spaces easier, since it protects you from oncoming cars.

- There are dips running across the streets that can fill up with water during a rainstorm. Be aware that the water can be deeper than expected, so approach slowly. Avoid driving through it, if possible. If you see a sign with the word *vado*, slow down. A dip in the road is just ahead.

- Some intersections do not have a stop sign, but there's a crosswalk. Look for pedestrians and stop as needed.

- When making a left-hand turn off the *Libre* or free road, if another car is behind you, don't just stop to make the turn assuming that the car behind will wait. Watch him. He may get into the pass lane on the left cutting you off to try to go around. It's common practice for those who are making the turn to get into the right-hand shoulder, wait for traffic behind to clear and then make the turn.

+ Although a fence is being erected as a divider between the southern and northern travelers on the toll road, a driver should be aware that a person or animal could dart across the road in his path at any given moment. Be particularly careful at night. People do not realize that dark clothes make them almost invisible in the dark. Sometimes a horrible accident occurs as a result of an innocent circumstance as the following story illustrates.

Señor P. is a family man who supported his family by driving his own water truck. While he was delivering water in one neighborhood, a little child somehow got caught beneath the tires of his truck without his knowledge while he was stopped. When he started his truck, the child was crushed by the tires, which killed him instantly. This tragedy devastated Señor P. both emotionally and financially, and he compensated the child's family with money from the sale of his truck, vowing never to drive a truck again.

What is the difference between the Cuota and Libre roads?

Anyone traveling south or north has the choice of the *Cuota* or *Libre* road. Each road has its purpose. The *Cuota* is a well-paved four-lane pay road with toll booths that will collect up to $2 from you (depending on peso valuation) each time you pass through. There are three toll booths on the *Cuota* between the border and Ensenada. Those who wish to travel quickly will prefer to pay instead of taking the free road that winds along the ocean shore. The *Libre* offers a selection of shops or restaurants along the way and continues into the mountains. However, the *Libre* or free road is not one to use after dark. It could be dangerous with all its twists and turns.

What does it mean when the driver in front turns on his left signal but doesn't turn?

The left turn signal may have two different meanings. It is up to the driver behind to interpret it by checking to see if there is a road to the left. If not, it could mean that it is safe to pass. Be very, very cautious with this signal. It is safer to trust on open highways than in city driving.

What does it mean if the driver in front blinks his right turn signal?

He may simply be making a right hand turn or he may be warning the car behind that it is **not** safe to pass.

What does it mean when an oncoming car turns his lights on and off?

It may be a warning to proceed with caution because some danger is ahead.

What dangers lurk on the roads of Baja California?

Unlike in the US, road workers may be exposed to oncoming traffic without a flagman to warn drivers of their presence ahead. They could be working into the evening hours when it's dark, so a driver needs to be cautious. There may be signs that read *Peligrosa. Hombres trabajando.* Translated they read Danger. Men working.

It's common to see fires along the sides of the roads. They're generally contained. Either they're used to heat the tar for the road or the brush is being burned purposely to control its growth.

Another surprise to a driver are roads that converge into one another unexpectedly, or three or more intersections which all converge. The best policy is to approach these areas cautiously. Once you become familiar with the roads, you will feel comfortable with them just like a local resident.

When you least expect it, there may be something crossing the road ahead. Cattle, horses or people may be on the road.

What is the *Tijuana Tingle*?

The **Tijuana Tingle**, according to Judy Sager, is the feeling you experience when you're driving in downtown Tijuana and all of a sudden you get caught in a swirl of traffic going around a statue of an Indian, scissors or statesman. It makes you break out in a sweat and tingle all over in a panic as you try to recall what you learned in the driver's training manual about traffic circles. You realize now that if you had studied better you'd know what to do, while the neighboring cars seem to squeeze into your territory as they manipulate themselves around your car and out of the circle. The tingle is the feeling of helplessness as the frenzy continues and there you are, going around and around until you have the nerve to make your own attempt to be assertive. Don't worry, by the third time around, you will have managed to watch how others exit and although it may not be where you wanted to go, you'll manage. After more experience in downtown Tijuana, you'll become an expert at traffic circles too. The Tijuana tingle will fade, but it's guaranteed you'll have the opportunity from time to time to watch it surface as some other inexperienced Tijuana driver has the privilege of experiencing the Tijuana tingle!

What else should I expect while driving in Tijuana?

♦ Until you become familiar with driving in Tijuana, always travel with a map of the downtown roads because the way in which the roads angle can be confusing.

♦ Expect to be accosted by "salesmen" on the road, especially when in a tourist area. Everything from coffee to brooms, cactus or seasonal goods such as Santa's hats could be offered to you to purchase while you wait at stop signs.

♦ Advertisements could pass by in the form of a voice or music through a bullhorn off the top of a truck or car, or perhaps on colorful written words or pictures on a traveling billboard cleverly attached to both sides of a glass truck.

- When searching for a parking area, be aware that there are parking lots which accept validation from nearby shops. They're not only free if you make a purchase but they're guarded, assuring your car is safe from theft. Sanborn's Department Store and Bazar de Mexico on Revolucion are examples of places which validate your parking in certain lots.

- In Tijuana the green traffic lights blink three times as a warning that they will turn to yellow, then to red.

- On certain corners in downtown Tijuana, pedestrians will cross kitty-corner, from corner-to-corner, European style.

What does the highway marker K-10 mean?

- It is a kilometer marker indicating the location on the highway. There are 112 kilometers or 70 miles between Tijuana and Ensenada. If a marker reads K-10 it means you're ten kilometers south of Tijuana. It's also used as an easy-to-find address. It can be confusing, however, because the toll road has different markers than the *Libre* road. It's very important to know which road is being described. Also, the counting starts over at Ensenada K-0 to San Quintin K-126. If I want to tell someone how to get to my home in Rosarito, I will say, "Go to K-38.5 on the *Libre* Road."

How do I recognize the difference between traffic road signs?

- **Restrictive** signs—are black or red on white background.

- **Preventive** signs—are black figures on yellow background.

♦ **Informational** signs—are white on blue background.

Why do the Baja California Mexican license plates read *Front*?

Front is the abbreviation for the word *Frontera*, meaning "frontier". Baja California is a peninsula that is considered to be very far away from the mainland of Mexico. It is considered to be a distant and faraway land or frontier, much the way Alaska is considered in the United States. Hence, the name on the license plates.

What services are there on toll roads?

The Secretary of Tourism says:

> Services offered along the Tijuana to Ensenada toll road include mechanical services which are provided by personnel who circulate from Tijuana to Ensenada. They will take care of emergency calls to repair vehicles on the toll road. They also offer medical services in Tijuana and Ensenada provided by qualified personnel. Ambulance service is also provided. For comfort the traveler can count on clean restrooms, a tourist information booth in Tijuana and Ensenada, and also public phones.

> Another service offered on this Federal toll road supporting your security is **America**, a free accident insurance policy in case you have one while driving on this road. The policy is automatic when paying the fees at each toll booth. Every kilometer and a half, emergency radio communications are provided.

Note: Save the current receipts from the toll booths or you won't be able to use this insurance. This shouldn't be considered a substitute for your personal Mexican insurance.

What does the toll road insurance policy cover?

◆ liability for third parties

◆ final costs

◆ medical costs

Who are the Green Angels?

The Mexican government provides help on the toll roads. The Secretary of Tourism states:

> This is an organization belonging to the Federal Secretary of Tourism whose main function is to help tourists in case they have any problem with their vehicle on the highway. They also provide mechanical service, which is free; they have a communication network with different government offices of the same branch that also offers basic information about the state and the rest of the country.

What is an *IAVE* card?

If you travel the toll road often, consider obtaining an *IAVE* card. It allows you to drive through a private express lane at the toll booth which lets you to pass without stopping. Charges are added to your credit card each time you go through the toll booth. A decal on your car window automatically activates a special automated lane. A 20% discount and roadside emergency service are extended to all who have cards. Call 888-USE-IAVE or (66) 30-80-27 for more information. Website: http://www.iave.com

Why do so many drivers honk horns in Mexico?

If you're planning to live in Mexico, it's necessary to practice your own signature honking technique that will express your personality. You could blast the horn, hit it lightly or rhythmically tap it to music. Of course if you're really clever, you could create your own code like the Morse code. If you desire to become an advanced horn blower you could install a custom horn that plays tunes or whatever you choose. You see, there's a difference between a Mexican's attitude toward horn blowing and that of his Northern counterpart. In the States a person might take it as an insult to have someone blaring a horn as you drive down the road, while the Mexican nature apparently gets some sort of pleasure out of the sounds. No one in Mexico will jump out of his car with a gun in anger, not only because possessing a gun is a felony but because no one gets angry over horn honking. Instead, any self-respecting Mexican citizen within hearing distance will enjoy the mixture of noises so much that he will join everyone else in a few lasting moments of a horn honking symphony.

How do local Mexican drivers react to foreigners who obviously are driving cars with an out-of-country license plate?

Drivers don't seem to mind sharing the road with foreigners

as long as they're driving in a *Mexicana* style that is direct and fast. Many tourists get lost, causing them to drive hesitantly while trying to figure out where they are. If local commuters are heading home they won't be rude; they'll just pass by quickly. Some kindly person may give directions or be otherwise helpful, but most will just go around the *turista*. Many times I've experienced other drivers assuming I'm slow and helpless because of my out-of-country license plates, but they soon learn I can keep up with them. Could there be a *macho* attitude in their behavior?

The first time in a year we met rudeness on the road occurred on a lonely, winding road heading toward the Tecate border. A car full of Mexicans passed us. We followed behind their car for awhile, but at one point Dick, my husband, who was driving, decided to pass them. Just as we started to move into the pass lane the other car suddenly swerved into our path. It was obvious we would have been rammed if Dick hadn't pulled back. He decided not to attempt to pass again. The driver's face in the side mirror had a big grin on it. Perhaps the *macho* driver was just having fun dominating *Gringos*. Like a practical joke that should cause me to laugh, but I can't find humor in it. In fact the incident has caused me to seriously consider going through the process of getting Mexican license plates and . . . perhaps . . . a can of pepper spray?

What are the general recommendations for driving from the Baja California Secretary of Tourism?

♦ Don't drink and drive.

♦ Always wear seat belts.

◆ Make certain your vehicle is in good mechanical condition.

◆ Obey all road signs and traffic laws.

◆ Don't leave valuables in a parked car.

◆ Always carry valid ID.

If I'm involved in a traffic accident, what do I do?

According to the Secretary of Tourism, if there are material damages you should:

◆ Wait at the location where the accident took place until the proper authority arrives.

◆ If your vehicle has insurance, notify your insurance company.

◆ If there are only superficial material damages, both parties may come to an agreement regarding payment for damages.

◆ If agreement cannot be reached or if damages are high, the case can be referred to the District Attorney's office.

◆ If the accident occurred on a Federal highway and the road suffered damages, the case is turned over to the Federal District Attorney's office.

For accidents in which there are substantial material damages or injured people, the involved parties may reach an agreement regarding damages. In relation to injuries, the case may be sent to the District Attorney, depending on the seriousness of the injuries. In order to make any claims for expenses caused by accidents, the injured party must have a medical certificate and hospitalization receipts and has to be under medical care. The responsible party will remain in the District Attorney's custody.

Why do people leave the scene of an accident before the police arrive?

This is against the rules, but many quickly settle disputes, deciding to pay for any damages themselves so they will not have their cars impounded or so they won't have to go to jail.

An excerpt from my journal indicates how three local Mexican citizens handled an accident:

> Today while eating lunch on the patio overlooking the ocean at Raul's Restaurant, I witnessed an automobile accident. Four roads intersect across the street from the restaurant. Three cars were converging at the same time. Two collided. The third car drove off without stopping. It made the quickest getaway I've ever seen. The drivers of the other two cars got out to examine the damage. They yelled at each other while making hand motions that indicated anger. Then, to my surprise, they each returned to their cars, leaving the scene of the accident. They evidently solved the problem them-selves, taking responsibility for the damage to their own cars. It doesn't cost a lot for auto body repair, so I guess they thought it wasn't worth taking the chance of having their cars impounded by the police.

Another accident was handled differently:

> Brian, an acquaintance, told me of a horrible accident that occurred as he was making a left-hand turn off the

free road into his driveway. Another driver who was passing illegally on the wrong side of the road plowed into him at a high speed. Brian was injured badly enough to go to the hospital while his car suffered extensive damage. The police consequently impounded both cars and the other driver was taken to jail for reckless driving. When I last saw Brian it was about a month after the accident. He still hadn't received his car from the police.

And lastly, there was this incident:

Yesterday I saw a car accident that was caused by a car trying to get on a ramp to the Ensenada Cuota at an unreasonable speed. Misjudging the curve, the driver hit a guardrail. This smashed the car enough to seriously injure a passenger who was trapped in the mangled wreck for over a half-hour while the police tried to get her free. When the police first arrived, handcuffs were immediately placed on the driver. With sirens blaring, an ambulance arrived; the injured party was placed on a stretcher in the back while another passenger joined the driver in the front seat to accompany his friend to the hospital. What was the fate of the driver? After the ambulance sped away, a policeman guided the careless driver to a waiting police car. The driver was on his way to jail.

CHAPTER FIVE

PEOPLE

**The simplicity of their lives and the happiness
their hearts can be felt by the most callused of souls.**

—Judy Sager
Popotla

What types of people reside in Northern Baja California?

Mexican people are warm and friendly. They value their families and they love children. The following is an excerpt from my journal:

The heartbeat of these people pulses with caring and warmth. My granddaughter Emma, who is one year old, crawled all over the beach the other day making friends with everyone along the way. I followed her closely as she headed to a group of young people who were sunning themselves next to us. Emma smiled at them, waved and instantly drew attention to herself. Her admirers appeared to be about 18-23 years old, both guys and gals. They laughed with glee at her every gesture and proclaimed that she was *muy hermosa*, or very pretty. They were genuinely delighted by this little baby girl, so much so that they allowed her to play with their plastic blow-up water shark for as long as she wished.

The phrase, *Mí casa es tu casa* translates to "My house is your house". Mexicans entertain guests in their homes with open hospitality. They love to sing and dance and will party until 6 AM. If you've never been to a Mexican *fiesta*, you've really missed a lot of fun. Don't go home too early!

The people of Baja California go out of their way to help. The other day I was lost in Tijuana because a detour led me into an unfamiliar area. I asked a person in a car next to mine for directions and he literally told me to follow him. He went out of his way to lead me to my destination! He wanted no more than a thank you and I didn't even know him!

There are approximately 45,000 Americans living between the US border and Ensenada. They have one thing in common. They are happy. Question them about their lives, and they say they'll never go back to live in the States. They have found a pleasant place to live. Why not? The ocean, weather and cost of living equal perfection. Their attitude of peace and tranquillity shows they're content.

What attitude should I have toward Mexicans?

Do not have negative feelings of fear or dislike or superiority toward them. Such negative feelings are unjustified and are based on prejudicial attitudes with no foundation in reality. Humbly observe the people and it will become apparent that they are friendly, happy and helpful. They're hard workers who know the value of relationships. They have a fierce sense of pride that flares when they're confronted with unreasonable demands. If you treat them fairly and warmly, they will treat you in the same manner. Rules of politeness should be observed by everyone, just as in the United States.

Mexican society is based upon a humble culture rooted in antiquity that teaches the principle of practicing graciousness in all social circumstances. The following words are taught at an early age when a person needs to excuse him/herself from joining others in a social or business event: *con su permiso* means "with your permission". A sense of humility expressed by polite manners is a valued attitude in Mexico.

Politeness and respect are social graces that are taught when Mexican children are little. I recently went to a college graduation *fiesta* where the male graduates wore tuxedos and the females wore fancy ball gowns. The graduating senior personally greeted each person who attended the party with respectful and polite formality. It was obvious she was grateful for the love and support of her family and friends. In a ceremony on stage parents were presented encrypted plaques as a thank you for supporting the graduates through college. It was touching to watch the youth joyously spend time dancing with their older relatives until

2 AM. The love they had for each other was evident in the rapport they openly displayed with one another.

What are some hints I should know about the cultural practice of being introduced to someone for the first time?

The words *mucho gusto* are often used with a handshake upon introduction of an individual. If there are others present, go around the table to greet each person individually.

When I greet someone I already know, what should I do?

The warmth and openness of the Mexican people are shown when they greet those they know on a personal basis. They will hug, possibly kiss the cheek, and ask *"cómo está"* which means "how are you"? They ask it as though they really care, and they do! If you're accepted as a close friend, it is for life, not for a passing whim. You have gained their trust and respect, which is a valuable gift.

An anecdote from my journal is as follows:

> I spent the evening with Linda Dobson in Ensenada. We attended a street fair in front of the San Tomas Winery as part of the annual Ensenada Wine Festival. It appeared that everyone, young and old, who lives in the town was there enjoying the festive activities. Throughout the evening Linda was constantly greeted by people with genuine facial expressions of delight. Warm hugs and kisses always followed the words,

"Linda, *cómo está*?" Great love and caring were poured out to her. She has lived in Ensenada for twenty years, speaks Spanish fluently and is a respected member of the community. This type of greeting happened with such regularity all through the evening that I felt as though I was with the mayor, or the queen of the ball.

What actions do Mexicans consider rude?

An act of rudeness occurs when a person compliments another too much. In Mexico a person is suspected of being insincere and is not trusted because he's *hechando demasiada crema* or "putting too much cream on the taco". It is believed that too much cream smothers the good taste of the taco. Subtlety and humility are more acceptable in the Mexican social culture than aggressive behavior, which is considered to be obnoxious.

If a person openly brags about his/her own accomplishments he/she is making a social breach that will leave him/her without the respect of others. Being thought of as *muy sensillo* or very simple is a compliment to a Mexican. Americans who practice assertiveness are considered to be boorish. Being candid, direct and quick to criticize are traits not appreciated nor respected by Mexicans. Mexican sense of pride can be injured if one doesn't understand that treating another with respect is more valued than openly voicing one's opinion, thus causing contention. Confrontation, verbal sparring and contention are rude behaviors that need to be avoided. In fact, if one uses sarcasm or explodes with anger toward another person, he loses his point or battle by virtue of his obnoxious behavior. Nothing may be said in retaliation at the time, but be assured the rude individual will either never be invited back or will be subtly treated to a passive-aggressive punishment. Americans need to understand the Mexican culture. It is the manner of the American that needs adjustment, not that of the Mexican. Patience, humility and graciousness are qualities Americans need to practice when dealing with Mexicans.

What are passive-aggressive ways?

Mexicans have a way of doing things on their own time schedules. Passive-aggressive behavior may consist of simply doing nothing. Although many times it's not intentional, there are times when situations are set up to drive the other person to anger. The person who sets it up retains the attitude of total innocence. For instance, a workman will not show up for a job at the scheduled time. If you get angry, he will not understand why you'd be so mad. In another case, if a disrespectful American snaps his fingers or whistles when he's ready for the bill in a restaurant, the waiter will slow down and ignore him, causing the rude person to fume, while the waiter carries on in apparent innocence.

Graham Mackintosh in his book *Into a Desert Place* describes an incident with Mexican fishermen when he helped them carry heavy boxes:

> The carrying was heavy, exhausting work. Three of us would take two crates up at a time. More often than not I found myself in the middle with a crate and an over-eager fisherman on either side. Everything was being done at a feverish, very un-Mexican pace. I felt sure they were testing me but I did my share without

complaint. Towards the end I was ready to drop but I wasn't going to show it. At last, with some satisfaction, I noticed the pace slackening. I had survived their playful onslaught and earned their respect.

Whatever else these fishermen were, they were *macho*—men and proud of it. Like fishermen everywhere they held in high regard the manly values of strength, courage and uncomplaining forbearance. To them I was an enigma, *el gringo loco*, the little redhead with big ideas. They wanted to know what I was made of.

What causes Mexicans to be stubborn and uncooperative when they're generally so friendly and helpful?

When treated fairly, they are hard workers, but a fierce sense of pride and stubbornness flares when an obnoxious person tries to bully or insult them. I recorded the following example of such behavior:

Tonight I saw an example of how some Mexicans handle a rude American. At the end of the evening the band had packed up all their instruments after playing music all night in a local bar. Mr. American came into the bar and insisted that they allow his friend to sing with the band's accompaniment. He was belligerent and very angry, saying, "This is the last time I'll ever come into this bar again," when they told him it would take too much time to unpack their instruments. They later told me they would have played for him if he had asked them in a polite manner. They didn't like the way they were treated. I didn't blame them.

What type of person would find it difficult to adjust to living in Baja California, Mexico?

Baja California is not for everyone. Those who are obsessive-compulsive about external perfection would have a difficult time adjusting to a non-materialistic, easy-going society.

One person described it in the following words:

> I'm starting to get used to the way things are done in this country. I have to lower my level of expectations or I would die of frustration. If I have ten things I need to get done during the day all of which would be possible to complete in the States with ease, I consider it a good day if three items on the list are accomplished. If the computer system isn't down, the person who runs it is sick or on leave. If we have electricity, the phone lines are all busy. It always seems to be one thing or another. The one thing you can count on is the person responsible for completing the work will have a good excuse!

How does Mexican cuisine relate to the Mexican personality?

The following words are taken from Nereyda, a 100% Latina member of the Cocina-Mexicana chat group that can be joined at cocina-mexicana@onelist.com:

> The richness of our cuisine flows from our concern for the sensory experience of eating, for we know that the taste, smell and look of food can enrich and inspire the spirit. It is often said that "cuisine is culture," and to

understand the development of Mexican cuisine is important to know something of the history of Mexico. In the pre-Colombian period, the diet of our Mexican ancestors was purely native with nutrition based on the great product of Mexican agriculture, corn. When thrashed and boiled into a *pozole*, the corn could be made into flavorful *tortillas* and *tamales*, or rendered into flour for other variations.

The diet of corn was supplemented with vegetables and meat. A great variety of spices, known as *chile*, could be combined with sweet potato, beans, squash, *chayote*, and *jicama*.

After the Conquest and during the Colonial Period, the country's cuisine changed dramatically with the culinary influences brought along by the Spanish. With the *conquistadores* and their descendants came a taste for *cabana*, for rice, olives, wines, spices from India, beef, and different kinds of fruit. Today's Mexican cuisine is a blend of the original Indian fare with the Spanish.

During the 19th century, Mexican women played a profound role in domestic life. To be a good woman in Mexico meant to have a profound knowledge and great skill in preparing the cuisine. The imagination, talent and gift for improvisation of the women of that period contributed much to the recipes that have been handed down to us. The demand for their delicious dishes around the world is a testament to them. Mexicans are very proud of their cuisine; to them it gives a sense of unity and identity everywhere in the world where they meet.

How do Mexican women differ from American women?

American women dress more casually than Mexican women. Generally, a Mexican woman will be well-groomed from head to toe, wearing nylons, full make-up and perhaps a hat when she goes out for the evening, while an American woman wears a simple dress or pants with sandals, no nylons. A young Mexican lady revealed she wished she could wear blue jeans the way American women do. She feels socially obligated to wear suits and dresses while American women can put on a simple jacket with blue jeans and be perfectly acceptable. If a man goes jogging along city streets without a shirt or if a woman exposes her cleavage, he or she is breaking the social code of modesty.

An excerpt from my journal indicates the difference:

> I went to a *fiesta* tonight which was a charity dinner-dance presented to the community by a Mexican landowners' organization. The tables were formally set with lovely flower arrangements on white linen tablecloths. A full live band played dance music while waiters dressed in black suits catered the gourmet food. Colorful helium balloons that were hanging above the outdoor dance floor enhanced the full moon and stars. It's interesting to note the difference between the American local residents and the Mexican residents in their attire. Many of the Americans were wearing T-shirts and jeans or jogging outfits, while Mexican men were dressed in suits and ties and Mexican women were wearing fancy evening dresses. The difference between the cultures was quite evident. I didn't understand why I was being mistaken for a Mexican until I

realized I was dressed up in a party dress, nylons and formal shoes much like the local Mexican landowners. I have great respect for a people who have a culture so full of dignity. It was evident that the party was prepared to be elegant. Isn't it interesting that the American locals apparently missed this nuance? I want to be a part of the Mexican culture. It's a compliment to be mistaken for a Mexican.

A Mexican woman may be educated to be a doctor, lawyer, dentist, architect etc., so don't underestimate her. She may have a full-time maid who does all the household chores. Her education and travel experiences may be far superior to yours. In fact, you may never see her since she sends her maids to shop for her and will never go into a local bar.

Ensenada women have gatherings that are not geared for tourists. In fact, the only way an American can be included is by special invitation. Recently, an auditorium was filled with women who gathered to enjoy a poetry reading of a fourteenth-century woman writer who was a free thinker. She was the first liberated woman to speak out. She had to join a monastery in order to write her philosophy in peace. Envision an auditorium full of well-dressed women. There's a hush in the room because one woman enters it from the back. She recites poetry as she continues down the aisle. When she reaches the stage, she joins a panel of other women who share their knowledge about the poetess. The condition of the times, the educational achievement and her philosophy are presented. This presentation lasted one and one-half hours, ending with a poem made into a song harmoniously sung by three ladies. Wine and cheese were elegantly served before the women departed.

A Mexican man may be educated to be a highly skilled doctor, lawyer, etc. Don't underestimate his polite manners. He may have more education and cultural dignity than you could ever imagine. Don't let an old cowboy hat and boots fool you!

My advice to you? Get rid of preconceived prejudices and silently observe these gracious people. You may learn a lot.

Jose Torres, a California man of Mexican descent, tells the following story:

> On a visit to Mexico, I was in a store trying on a Mexican hat and colorful serape. As I was admiring myself in the mirror, a couple of American tourists asked me if they could take my picture. I posed for them, changing positions while practicing my broadest smile. When they finished they seemed pleased as they handed me some money saying, "Thanks for the pictures. We really appreciate being able to take a picture of an authentic Mexican." I replied, "I'm not a Mexican. I'm a California boy, born in the United States, just here on vacation." I guess they thought Mexicans still wear serapes and Mexican hats, because they were obviously startled. I, of course, was highly amused.

Are Mexicans clever at fixing things?

Mexicans are ingenious at fixing a problem. They'll put a lot of thought into solving problems creatively as this story from Linda Dobson illustrates:

> The most clever solution to a problem in construction

I've seen was in a house that was for sale in Mexico. The door to the bathroom must not have been closing after the toilet was installed because the builder cut out a piece of the door so it would clear the toilet upon opening. When the door closed, the cutout joined a piece on the door jam that fit into the hole like a jigsaw puzzle. When opened, the door with its cutout cleared the toilet. I can just envision the builder mulling the problem over in his head until he came up with that idea. The important thing is that his idea worked just fine.

Judy Sager, Kathy Wasson and I had an experience in a restaurant that illustrates a simple solution to a problem. We ordered lunch in a Tijuana restaurant. When we told the waiter we needed a spoon for our salsa, he quickly solved the problem by removing the spoon from the butter dish and placing it in the salsa. No problem. We had the spoon for the salsa. Oh well, one spoon is as good as another!

Adolfo Kim's reaction to stress is, "Roberta, relax, you are now in Mexico. There are no problems!"

Indeed, during New Year's weekend, businesses were closed not for one day, but for the entire weekend. One young man told us that he was planning to take his wife out for New Year's Eve to dance until 6AM at which time they all planned to have breakfast at a relative's home before leaving to spend the day picnicking in the mountains. They'd go without sleep and make up for it another day. Hence, the entire weekend was a celebration. Business and responsibilities would be put on hold until it was over.

A neighboring house in San Antonio Del Mar has an electric box cover that is often left open. I have a good chuckle as I drive by. Some enterprising person needed to build a cover for the electric box, so he borrowed the lumber to create it from a real estate sign. On the inside of the box is the logo and name of a local real estate office. No wonder we keep losing our Re/Max signs! They've been "borrowed" to be cleverly recycled. I had an idea that we should switch to vinyl signs until I saw a stack of hay covered with what should have been tarp but was a collection of colorful vinyl signs. Oh well, maybe my name will be flapping in the wind somewhere and make me famous in Mexico.

Jack Smith, in his book *God and Mr. Gomez*, offers another example of how Mexicans can fix things by the cannibalization of cars:

> For years the transport of Baja had survived by the interchangeability of parts. Ford and the Chevrolet were standard. The peninsula was strewn with their carcasses, but not a part was wasted. Every detachable organ was cannibalized and put back into the mainstream.

If a car breaks down a Mexican mechanic can borrow parts from another to fix it. There are many cannibalized wrecks available for such repairs.

Be careful: If you have a foreign car for which parts are not easily accessible, the use of common parts could cause more damage than the original problem. Make certain the mechanic specializes in your type of car.

Describe some of the people who live in Baja California.

Certainly, there are a variety of colorful characters who choose to live in Baja California. Meet the following:

Adolfo Kim

Adolfo Kim is a native of Tijuana who lives in Rosarito. He taught a class to Americans who wanted to learn to speak the Spanish language. He's a precise teacher who would go around the room making each of us pronounce first the sounds, then the words, coaching us to repeat them until they were uttered like a native. Sometimes we were painfully embarrassed, but the end result is that we now have an excellent foundation. He's a proficient teacher who taught us a lot more than Spanish. He cooked meals for us, took us on field trips to Ensenada and Tijuana and taught us how to take the local bus, all because he wanted us to become self-sufficient in this foreign country. We learned the innuendos of the culture.

He told us to call him whenever we needed him. If we need help translating Spanish or if we get into accidents or if our roofs leak, he's there to help. It works in the reverse too because he's needed help from us. He's a hard worker, so when he stopped teaching Spanish lessons, he started a home maintenance business. We hired him and got him enough jobs with our friends so he's very busy now. He's building a new home, paying as he goes. First, he purchased the land. He fenced it next securely enclosing a trailer where he lives with his wife and two daughters. The foundation for a new house is poured but the studs will have to wait until he makes enough money to install them. The house will go up bit by bit over time as he makes the money to complete it.

He says to me when I express concern over finances, "Roberta, you worry too much about money." He exemplifies the Mexican ability to enjoy the moment, having faith that tomorrow will take care of itself. The building of his house is envisioned in his mind as a certainty. The combination of his determined faith and feisty pluck will cause it to happen; but in the meantime, he will enjoy the moment while it is here, for tomorrow has not yet arrived.

Judy Sager recalls the following incident. It illustrates Adolfo Kim's ability to forge ahead even in the face of adversity:

> Members of our Spanish class who met at René's Restaurant three times a week were anticipating an outing in the fresh air to visit local nurseries. We wanted to know where to find lovely cut flowers for bargain prices. The women in the class looked forward to colorful fresh flowers to decorate our homes every day. When I looked out the window the morning of the scheduled tour, I saw a relentless *El Niño* rainstorm. Good common sense dictated that I should stay in my warm, dry home, but not wanting to be considered a flake, I dressed as warmly as I could and headed out in the downpour.
>
> When we met at René's, I was amazed to see that no one else stayed home. I thought Adolfo would postpone the outing to another day, a dry one. No such luck. He smiled excitedly stating that the rain just added a sense of adventure to our outing. Because we couldn't all fit

into one car, I rode in a van with other members of the class. We followed Adolfo south on the free road toward the nurseries. The rain continued in such a heavy downpour that our windshield wipers couldn't go fast enough to give us clear vision. Yet we continued to follow Adolfo's car as it sloshed ahead.

It's difficult to describe the road conditions, but I'll try. Wherever the road dipped, water gathered into what seemed like fast running streams that we'd have to cross. Each time we'd come to one, I'd hold my breath hoping the car would make it across safely, not getting swept away by the swiftly moving water. When we'd make it to the other side we cheered with relief. We finally arrived at the nurseries ready to wade through thick, gooey mud that splattered over our soaked feet and legs. We were miserable with wet, muddy hair and clothes. Adolfo, just as wet and muddy as we were, was cheerful and unfazed, acting as though nothing unusual was happening. So what's a little wet mud? Even when we watched a bridge wash away blocking our approach to another nursery, he didn't turn back. He just found a different route to travel.

I'll never forget that day when we all thought our lives were in danger but Adolfo had the calm attitude of acceptance. "We're watched over by God. He's our friend," he said with a shrug of his shoulders. He was right. We made it home safely taking with us a memory of forging through the *El Niño* waters from heaven to look at flowers.

Jesus Navarro Valdez

Jesus Valdez owns a wonderful shop in town, called *Casa de Flores*. He's an intuitive person who recognizes the depth in people. He instantly shows warmth to those who come into his shop. When he first met me, he said in reference to astrology, "You're a Libra." He was correct! Since then he's introduced me to several potential clients, thereby helping me build my real estate business in Mexico. One time he introduced me to a person with whom he thought I could network. When this person and I discovered we had our birthdays in common, we were flabbergasted at Jesus' insight. It was a twilight zone moment of discovery in our lives! Go visit him in his store located across the street from the La Quinta Plaza in Rosarito on the main street. Maybe he'll have insights for you too!

Joel Villavicencio

Joel lives with his family in Bahía de Los Angeles. He lives a life in the sun and sea because he's a fisherman who takes tourists out for cruises and/or for sport fishing on the Sea of Cortez. He enjoys cruising to a bay where a person can swim with harmless sharks who eat plankton, not meat. Many tourists ask him to take photographs while they swim with the sharks.

He has taught his son, who is 11, to be his first mate on the boat. It's heartwarming to watch the son obey his father without complaint. While relaxing, the son will sit next to his dad with his head on his shoulder, or with one arm wrapped around him. While working, the son will suddenly burst out singing without self-consciousness, displaying an innocent contentment with life. His heart radiates peaceful love. He attends school so he isn't with his dad all the time, but the relationship is obviously close.

I witnessed an identical harmony between three generations of the same family. The grandfather, the father and the son all worked as a team when they had a flat tire on their pickup truck. The tire was changed in less than three minutes. It was the grandfather who gave the instructions. One person loosened the lug nuts while another jacked up the tire and so forth until the job was complete. There were no complaints, no hesitation and no fuss. It was a harmonious team working together for the good of all. Their warmth for each other overflows to everyone around them. Joel says to me, "You now have a friend in Bahía de Los Angeles." You can feel their warmth also if you go to Bahía de Los Angeles; look up Joel. He lives across the street from the museum. There's only one telephone in town, so leave a message. You won't be sorry. Call (011-52-166) 50-32-06 or -07.

Andrés Meling

Andrés Meling is one of the few remaining Baja California *vaqueros* or cowboys in Mexico. Born in 1926 to a Norwegian father and Danish mother, he was raised with four siblings on 10,000 acres, the Meling Ranch, located in a remote Mexican valley which lies between the highest mountain peaks of the Pedro Mártir in Baja California, Mexico. "If you want money, you have to work for it," Andrés' dad, who found gold in the mountains, taught the children at an early age. Each child, even the two girls, learned how to raise, rope, brand and care for over 2000 open-range cattle that had to be driven on horseback into the 9200-foot-high mountains during the summer and back to the 6200-foot valley for the winter. While they were growing up, the children had a live-in private tutor who taught them how to read and write in both English and Spanish. Life in the mountains was rough. The family suffered a tragic loss when a frisky horse fell upon Andrés' brother, crushing him to death at age 11.

Twice a year, food supplies were obtained by taking a four to five-day trip to town in a buggy with six horses. The nearest neighbor was eight miles away from the ranch. In 1940 the first car, a Chevy Coupe bought by the Melings, made it up the mountain by using the dry river bottom as a road. The family finally graded a rough dirt road in 1946. When the University of Mexico City Observatory was built on the highest peak in 1978, the government put in a road that passed the ranch, causing it to be accessible to the many guests who visit the ranch each year. An airport was later added, opening up to wealthy guests who visited Baja California as a playground for their indulgence. Horse packing trips into the mountains were adventurous outings arranged and guided by Andrés Meling.

Andrés remembers when he was contracted by ranchers to catch wild steers that had grown to at least 2000 pounds over two seasons without ever seeing man. The cowboys would have to travel into mountain plateaus that were so dense with scrub oak trees they could hardly ride through to catch the elusive cattle that would go down into the mesquite trees, rock piles or cat claw cactus and then back up again to escape capture. Their feet were as big as dinner plates and their horns were heavy and long like Texas Longhorns.

Andrés says:

A bull could pick you up, horse and all, if it gets underneath. I've never seen anyone killed, but mauled? Yes. I've had to pull a person away from being stomped and ground to death. When we were finally successful at lassoing them, their horns would immediately be sawed off in order to protect us from a brutal gouging. Their feet would be tied together. Big steers and bulls would be tied by rope around a tree to calm them down. We'd leave them that way for 24 hours to cool off; then they could be led like a horse to a corral. One time, while roping a big one, the rope accidentally wrapped around my saddle hand. Each time the bull charged, I could feel my bones cracking until every bone in my fingers was broken. The rope was skinning my hand until it was raw and bleeding. Within minutes, another cowboy appeared to help until all seven were there to subdue the wild animal. When they freed me, I cut the remaining skin off my hand, found a lumboy tree, which looks like a scrub apple tree, and proceeded to squeeze the juice of a branch onto the raw injury. I wrapped each finger in gauze and proceeded to squeeze the juice over the hand for hours all through the night. It foamed like peroxide and killed the pain. The next day we rode into Bahía de Los Angeles to catch a private plane to Tijuana. Two days after the accident, I finally arrived at the doctor's office in Tijuana. When the doctor removed the gauze, he found no infection. There were no scars. The lumboy plant, a favorite medicine of Baja California Indians, only grows south of Punta Piédra on the Baja Peninsula. It had worked its magic on my hand. (For another Andrés Meling story, see, page 233.)

Note: Those who wish to make reservations to stay at the ranch, which has been closed temporarily, may call (011-52) 617-75-897 for updated information.

Miguel De Hoyos

Miguel De Hoyos is touted to be the best classical guitarist in all of Baja California, Mexico, if not in all of Mexico. He plays in three or four night spots in Rosarito and occasionally in concerts in the United States. Jon'a F. Meyer states in the *Baja Sun* newspaper, "Miguel's skills were readily apparent . . . . His melodic poems take on their own lives, and flourish separately from both Miguel and his guitar . . . . He played classical music, folk tunes from around the world, traditional Mexican and Hispanic ballads, and even simulated a banjo duel between himself and his steadfast guitar . . . during the fast-paced flamenco pieces, Miguel's fingers flew like a hungry octopus in search of a meal . . . (the octopus) became more passionate until its fleeting tentacles could not be seen by the human eye." If you want to hear him in person, come to Rosarito. If you want more information or to order a CD for soothing background music, contact his manager, whose E-mail address is: lauramiller70@hotmail.com. (See page 289 for clubs in which he performs.)

Mama Espinoza

Mama Espinoza is a Baja California, Mexico, celebrity who has lived in El Rosario for most of her life. Born in El Rosario in 1908 as Anita Grosso, she later married Heraclio de Espinoza, a ranchero cowboy who fathered her ten children. Her humble life has been devoted to helping others, especially the poor and destitute who live in her little *pueblo* of El Rosario. Visit her restaurant located just south of the PeMex gas station as you enter the town. The food is excellent, the historical artifacts are mind boggling and the autobiographical book called *Reflections* by Mama Espinoza is a treasure to add to your personal Baja California library. It's filled with historical richness and examples of the strong, abiding faith of this remarkable lady whose life in El Rosario spans a century of faithfully serving her God and His children in Baja California, Mexico. It costs $10. She explains that half the proceeds go to charity and the other half to her sustenance. To order the book call: (011-52-616) 58770. If you wish to contribute clothes, blankets, food or money to her charitable cause, just leave it at the restaurant as you pass through town. If you happen to meet her, Mama Espinoza will leave you in awe of her resilience and devotion to the poor of her little *pueblo*. She will also give you the blessing in Spanish, *"Vayan con Diós,"* meaning "Go with God." Indeed, after my visit with her, I felt I had been in the presence of one of God's angels on earth and I knew I'd "go with God" because I left with the inspiration of this humble lady in my heart. (See page 278 for a description of how the Flying Samaritans began at Mama Espinoza's kitchen table.)

Those who are from the United States find Mexico to be a haven from their vigorous former lives:

Bill Sager

Bill Sager, a retiree, quietly lives in a house on the beach. When he came to Mexico, he could barely walk. His health is constantly improving as he breathes the fresh Baja

California air and power-walks around his campo. He's recovering from working for over fifty years as owner of the Buck Horn, a lodge on Mount Baldy in California; but he has a past that is even more colorful. He was the personal photographer for General MacArthur during World War II. His stories describe Tokyo, Japan, after the bomb was dropped on Hiroshima because he was assigned to photograph the signing of the armistice, or they reflect the horror of fighting in bloody battlefields. One time during the war his group found a deserted town in which there was a trunk left behind. They were dazzled to find it was full of shiny Japanese coins. It was a fortune! They were tempted to take it, but carrying it was not practical so they just left it behind. To listen to this man is to learn history from someone who lived it!

What does the term Mack-Spotting mean in Baja California, Mexico?

The term **Mack-Spotting** was coined when Graham Mackintosh, a red-haired Englishman, walked through Baja California, Mexico, on his treks down the coastline in the early eighties and then across the mountain tops with a burro in the nineties. He faced rattlesnakes, impenetrable terrain and unrelenting sunshine but overcame nature's obstacles with limitless courage. Mack-Spotting became a sport of the locals. If anyone saw him, he would be spotting Mack, the walking *loco* or crazy Englishman who later wrote a book about his adventures, called *Into a Desert Place*. The spottings became a verbal accounting of the progress of his journey. Because of these spottings, local residents knew when to anticipate his arrival as he traveled southward. Many had pictures taken with him. He became a celebrity legend in Baja California, Mexico, and received an award in London recognizing him as the *"Adventurous Traveller of the Year."* As I stopped at certain spots while traveling south such as the Cielito Lindo Motel in San Quintin or at the Costa del Sol Hotel in the town of Bahía de Los Angeles, I was able to discuss his trek with those who were doing the Mack-Spotting during those years. If you haven't read his book, I highly recommend it. His ability to describe his adventures is excellent, and the information it contains offers invaluable insights into the people, culture and terrain of Baja California, Mexico. It can be ordered from W.W. Norton in paperback for $15.95.

Who are the *snowbirds*?

The **snowbirds** are people who come south to Baja California during the winter when the state or country in which they live is cold. They "fly" south in their RV rigs to find the sun. They stay in Mexico from October until March to enjoy life in better weather. They can be seen traveling in caravans heading south to Baja California del Sur or they may settle in Baja California until they head back north in March. Look at their license plates to see where they're from. Such states as Michigan, Illinois, Connecticut, Oregon, Washington and the country of Canada are all represented. They come and go every year just like the birds who fly south during the winter; hence, they are the snowbirds.

Who are the *slinky people?*

Remember the coiled-wire toy that would go down one step at a time when set at the top of the stairs? The weight of the lower portion would pull the back part down to the next step. It would travel all the way down to the landing on its own volition. The **slinky people** are those who come to Mexico but never stay for very long because they're off to somewhere else. They're happy wherever they are. They possibly have another house in Palm Springs or at Lake Tahoe or somewhere, but they never stay in one or the other for very long. They differ from the snowbirds because they're so unpredictable.

How did US citizens get the name *gringos?*

This slang term has been used in reference to United States citizens for years. Its origin has three possible explanations. The most popular theory has to do with the green military outfits worn by the 10,000 soldiers who went across the border into Mexico in pursuit of Pancho Villa after he raided and murdered US citizens in Columbus, New Mexico. The US soldiers, under General John J. Pershing, returned home after an eleven-month fruitless search. Meanwhile, among the Mexicans, Pancho Villa was hailed as a national hero who was the only leader who "invaded" the United States. They wanted the US soldiers to leave their country so they shouted, "Green, go home," that turned into *gringo.*

In Spain during the late 18th century, the word *griego*, derived from the Greek language meant *foreigner*. Through the years it could have evolved into *gringo*.

United States soldiers sang a song, *Green Grow the Lilacs,* that was popular during the Mexican-American war. The first two words, "green grow," apparently were associated so much with the soldiers that they were eventually identified as *gringos* by the Mexicans.

Choose your favorite. Any one of these explanations could be true.

Who are the Yo-Yos?

Yo-Yo is the term Baja California Mexicans use in reference to people from Mexico City. The nickname is one that describes an arrogant person who is overly concerned with I, which is the meaning of the Spanish word *Yo*.

Can a single person experience a positive life in Baja California?

Yes. There are many singles living in Baja California, Mexico. Something magical occurs among the people of Baja California. They take care of each other. A person can determine what he/she wants out of life and then go after it. Golf, tennis, card games, dancing, fishing or simply watching the sunsets are available activities. There are book exchange or theater groups of people who all have something in common. They have fun together. On holidays, no one is alone unless solitude is desired. I know of a woman who is still surfing in her 60s or another 70-year-old who dances all night long. She says she has never had so much fun in all her life. I've met a widower whose taste in exquisite art is reflected all through his lovely home on an oceanfront. He has the greenest, most flourishing courtyard garden I've seen in this area. I've also seen the alcoholics who return every day to the same barstools to drink their lives away. Each is pursuing his/her own life in the way he/she chooses.

Some find the love of their lives. One real estate agent took off to live in Mulege with a Mexican lover, another woman in her 60s met a 30-year-old man and married him. Others fall in love down here and have weddings in quaint little hillside churches by the ocean. Still others are happy being single. Walking along the beach alone can be an exciting adventure. There are sunsets to enjoy, birds to watch and sand piles to wiggle through in bare feet. There are songs to sing and food to cook and people to help. Most people who live here are those who have a taste for the adventurous life. They have a spunk that brought them here in the first place. Many people say, "I'll never go back to live in the States. This is my home."

Jerry has an interesting story. He says he moved to Rosarito to start a new life after ending a 25-year marriage to a woman who was an alcoholic. He was not looking for a new wife; in fact, he didn't really want a new woman in his life, but during the course of his single days in Mexico, he met a Mexican *señorita* with whom he later fell in love. It is one of those coincidental occurrences that just happened because she worked as a caretaker for an elderly Chinese man who lived in a condominium unit below Jerry's. When Jerry took walks on the beach, he'd see this little Mexican lady sitting on the patio eating her lunch. He started casual conversations with her as a good neighbor, commenting on the weather or the sunsets or whatever neighbors discuss when they see each other.

Soon he found himself enjoying his encounters with her. Her laugh and her long dark hair started to capture him. He surprised himself one day when he asked her out to dinner. Yes, he enjoyed being with her. Even though her age at 34 and his at 66 could have been a major stumbling block to a relationship, he found they had much in common. After a while, he found himself proposing marriage to her. She accepted, so now he's married again. She rubs his back, cooks delicious meals for him and yes, he keeps up with her in the bedroom. He says he never smoked nor drank so his body functions like a younger man. It's the best sex ever! He's very happy. So is Juanita. She enjoys traveling with him and is rapidly adjusting to American ways. The American women who know them tease him by threatening to teach her how we handle our men. He wants her just the way she is, thank you!

Friends Across the Border is a multinational, confidential program which acts as a catalyst to help singles find partners who have similar interests. Cost is $10. Write to **Friends Across the Border** 858 Third Ave., Ste 456 Chula Vista, Calif. 91911-1305

Check out the Internet site with the words, girlsofsonora.com. It's a dating service in which a guy can access a video interview of different girls in order to select one to date. Why aren't there ever sites offering men for women to date? Let me know if you find one!

To marry in Mexico or to gain resident or immigration status for a non-US citizen fiancé(e), look up this Internet site: http://www.usembassy.org.mx/eacsinfo.html

C H A P T E R   S I X

SHOPPING AND SERVICES

When contracting a service or buying any product, verify the established conditions and require the corresponding invoice or receipt.
—Secretary of Tourism
Baja California, Mexico

Can I trust local service people to stand behind their work?

Yes. Mexican mechanics are noted for excellent work. Specialized shops can be found in any town including Rosarito. There are auto electric shops, muffler garages,

brake specialists and tire shops. Get reliable recommendations before you leave your car; then carefully negotiate
prices before the work begins. If the final bill exceeds 10%,
question it. There's probably a justifiable reason but if not,
it should be adjusted accordingly. Don't pay for a service
prior to completion. Only give payment to the principal
and always get a receipt. Such personal policies will prevent problems before they occur. I recommend taking a
local Mexican friend with you on the first visit. An introduction by a known local person will assure you of being
treated as a local, not a tourist. Because tourists are not
always respected, you may be charged a higher price. The
local person will offer credibility.

What is the purpose of the Federal Agency for Consumer Affairs?

This agency is responsible for assuring that the official prices
of basic food products and other items are respected. It promotes and protects consumer rights, and resolves conflicts
between consumers and suppliers of goods and services.

When purchasing a product or hiring out a service, you
must assure yourself that it is in good condition and you
should request a receipt, invoice or purchase order that
proves your payment of the service or acquisition of the
product.

The *Procuraduria Federal del Consumidor* (Federal Agency
for Consumer Affairs) is responsible for assisting you in
case a product or service provided by hotels, travel agencies or restaurants in tourist areas does not comply with
stipulations. Call (011-52-5) 710-5749.

To contact an American Embassy concerning consumer affairs in Mexico, call (011-52-66) 81-74-00. The American Embassy will assist you in pursuing a consumer complaint.

What is a duty-free zone?

When Baja California Norte is called a free zone, it means that it is a duty-free zone. The Mexican government allows imported items from around the world to be sold without the import taxes. This amounts to 20-50% savings on such items as perfumes, crystals, jewelry and brand-name clothing. Many stores in Tijuana offer such products. My favorites are Sanborn's Department Store, Maxim's and Sara's, all located on Revolution Avenue. The following is an excerpt from my journal:

> Today I visited **Sanborn's Department Store**. A high-class department store filled with exquisite items that can tempt even the most resistant shoppers, it offers validated parking below and a restaurant within. For a person whose tastes relish finer quality items, it's a virtual smorgasbord of goods. Toys, candy, books and purses are displayed for purchase. I found lovely baby dolls with sweet faces and snuggly bodies for my granddaughter. They're dressed beautifully in cotton gowns, straw hats and patent shoes. They cost $35 each. In the states they would cost $100 but I wouldn't be able to find such lovely dolls there.

Note: When I took the dolls for my granddaughters on the plane, they were hanging out of a shopping bag carry-on. Everyone who saw them stopped to ask me where I purchased such lovely dolls? It was a pleasure to answer, "at

Sanborn's in Tijuana" because most people don't know Tijuana offers such tasteful items that are much more than insignificant trinkets.

Where are the duty-free stores located in San Ysidro, California?

For those who are entering Mexico, the duty-free stores in San Ysidro offer considerable savings on designer perfumes, liquor, cigarettes and jewelry and leather handbags. Items are sold with substantial discounts on the condition they'll be taken directly into Mexico. You will be followed to the border after purchases are made. Many of the residents of Baja California will stop at the following stores on each return to Mexico in order to take advantage of the savings:

Ueta Duty Free Shops, (619) 428-4444, and **Baja Duty Free Shops**, (619) 428-6671, are located on the same block off San Ysidro Blvd. and Virginia St. on Border Village Road.

The option to leave a purchase in the store to be claimed and added to the $400 exemption allowed at customs on return to the United States is available.

Is negotiating the price acceptable in the marketplace?

In the stores mentioned above, the prices are marked and fixed. However, in most tourist stores along Revolution Avenue in Tijuana and in booths in Rosarito, it is possible to bargain. The first price offered is not the lowest. If you respond with a value of half that price, the merchant will probably split the difference. Sometimes I end up buying something I had no intention of purchasing, because the bottom line price is so good and the negotiating is so much fun. The following incident illustrates this:

> I went into Tijuana to accompany my friend Judy while she purchased a wedding present for a friend. As we walked through some booths on the way to the store, I stopped to look at a leather purse that caught my eye. The saleslady said the price was $45. I said, "Thank you," and started to walk away. She immediately said, "You can buy it for $35." I said, "No, thank you," and started to walk away again. She then came down to $25, a price that sounded very good to me. I said, "How about $23?" She agreed and I walked away with a birthday present for my daughter-in-law. I wasn't looking for a gift at that time, so I became a good negotiator without knowing it. If I had been looking for the purse, I probably would have thought the $35 was a bargain.

Is there handicapped access to stores, restaurants and businesses?

Unfortunately, it is uncommon in Baja California to find wheelchair access for public use. In Tijuana and Rosarito a few sidewalks have cutouts for wheelchairs, but the condition of the sidewalks is hazardous. There could be uneven pavement, unrepaired holes and any number of obstacles along the way. An unseen step could be the cause of an unexpected accident. Don't expect to receive any compensation for such negligence. Litigation for such matters is not common practice.

There's good news from Ensenada! The roads and side-walks along the popular shopping area have been totally redone so that there are smooth, wide sidewalks with curb cutouts for wheelchairs.

Is it possible to package and ship items home?

Yes. Some of the more expensive stores offer such a service, and there are specialized package shippers that will provide the service if you bring purchased items to them.

Mail Express in Rosarito, located across the street from the Rosarito Hotel, is a shipping outlet. Call (011-52-661)-2-2423.

Pro-Pack in San Ysidro, California, will ship large items such as furniture and iron items, or fragile goods. Located next to the US customs exit, next to Greyhound, their motto is, *"You buy it . . . we'll get it home!"* Call for more information: (619) 690-9558.

Should I shop locally?

A local resident from the US has the following philosophy:

> I support the local shopkeepers by avoiding purchasing outside the town. My goal is to find stores here that will meet my needs. A good rapport with local merchants never hurts anyone. Besides, they work hard to make a dollar. Why should money go elsewhere? I don't want to be like so many others who always have to run to the States to shop. Every need we have can be met right here.

What part of Rosarito offers good shopping?

Rosarito offers shopping on its main street near the Rosarito Hotel, located on the south end of town. This is the area the tourists choose to investigate for shopping. The locals, however, are aware of the many quality stores with excellent products at the middle and north ends of town. They are becoming more popular. Check them out. You may prefer to shop there too.

Which supermarket is the best to use?

I like to use the **Comercial** in Rosarito. It has a wonderful bakery with everything from fresh tortillas to delicious cookies and breads. It offers fruits and vegetables for half price on Tuesdays. It also has a pharmacy that offers discounts. It even sells clothes and household goods. It's located in a shopping center behind the **PeMex** gas station on the main street of Rosarito. Look for the orange pelican, its logo, in many Baja California Mexican towns.

Another supermarket chain, **Calimax**, has 35 stores in Baja California, Mexico. Located on 10th Street in Tijuana and the main street in Rosarito, the stores offer produce, liquor, meats and gourmet coffees.

Note: Ensenada has a supermarket called **Gigante** that is a fine market, but unfortunately it's necessary to give this warning. Many people have reported that their car gets stolen in the parking lot of one of its most popular supermarkets located on the route southward. Do not leave a car unattended in the parking lot in the shopping center where this supermarket is located unless you have an engine cut-off switch. Even with the cut-off switch, you should back into the parking spot so that your car can't be towed. Hopefully, this problem will get solved soon, but in the meantime, be careful.

Where do I purchase baguettes and other pastries?

La Baguette sells delicious baguettes, pies, cakes and cookies. Don't miss it! It's located on Blvd. Lázaro Cárdenas #1030, Ensenada, B.C. Phone: 61-78-28-14.

What wineries can I visit in Baja California?

90% of Mexico's fine wines are produced in the Guadalupe Valley near Ensenada, an area appropriately called the **Bordeaux Belt**. Tours and wine tasting are offered at each. The following are the most popular:

Bodegas de Santo Tomás—(011-52-617) 83333—Visit the **La Esquina De Bodegas** or **Corner at Bodegas** where a bookstore, café and wine bar, art gallery, gift shop and wine tasting are offered. Call (011-52-617) 40-807.

Bodegas San Antonio—(617) 83939
Casa Domecq—(66) 232171
Cavas Valmar—(617) 86405
L.A. Cetto—(66) 853031
Mogor Badan—(617) 71484
Monte Xanic—(011-52-617) 46-155"—"*A benchmark for the character and quality of wines made in the valle de Guadalupe*"

What items should I buy as gifts?

There are too many items to list, but my favorites are:

- **Piñatas**—There are many sizes and shapes. Nothing is more fun at birthday parties than to having the children try to break one open for the candy and prizes inside.

- **Clowns**—Brightly painted clowns that are tastefully made add a festive touch to a child's room.

- **Dice**—Marked with the same symbols found on a deck of cards, they can be used to play poker by shaking them as in a game of dice.

- **Onyx chess set** or **domino set**

- **Clay pottery**—everything from large flower pots to sun faces.

- **Rustic outdoor furniture**

- **Glass vases**

- **Oil paintings**—copies of famous works or of a favorite photograph

- **Leather** items—purses, wallets, jackets, etc.

It's possible to purchase all of the above items for reasonable prices in booths along the free road just south of Rosarito near the Fox Studio. However, stores in town are more likely to stand behind their products.

There's an open-air market located behind the stores on the main street through an alley just north of the El Nido Restaurant.

What items can I find and enjoy in Mexico that I can't bring to the US?

- Cuban cigars are sold and smoked freely in Mexico. Don't try to bring them across the border unless you enjoy the inside of an American jail.

- Some medicines that are not approved by the FDA or require a prescription in the US.

- Turtle products—Such as leather boots, tortoiseshell jewelry and oil-based cosmetics.

- Black coral items including jewelry.

- Spotted cat fur.

- Fireworks—Many fireworks that are banned in the states are allowed in Mexico.

- Parrots, stuffed or alive—Trying to import them into the States results in a jail term and a large fine.

- Switchblades and butterfly knives.

- Stuffed iguanas.

Where do I find excellent Mexican art?

There are several art galleries in Rosarito, but my favorite is the newest one called **Polo's Gallery**, located at K-33.5 south of town across from the 20th Century Fox Studios. Such talented artists as Rocio Hoffman, Armando Becerril Becris and Manuel Lizarraga have their works on display and for sale. Polo Valencia, gallery director, says he has "art that dazzles you with its color and content, art that leaves you in awe of the artist's skill and insight, representational art that you can appreciate, the best landscapes, seascapes, genre paintings, watercolors and drawings, by leading artists." Tell Polo "Roberta sent me," and he'll probably give you a discount.

Ray Martinez Gallery, located at K-33.5 across from the Fox Studio, carries oil paintings as well as wood and iron craft. Copies of famous oils or favorite photos can be made. Prices are reasonable. Ask for Henry. Call (011-52-66) 82-52-73 for more information.

George Santini Fine Art Gallery is located at K-40 on the free road south of Rosarito. Baja artists have quality art work on display for your pleasure.

Elvia Tadeo an artist who has a portfolio of original Mexican pastels will do commissioned artwork. She is a daughter of Mr. and Mrs. Andrés Meling, and descendant of prominent Mexican cattlemen and business people. Miss Tadeo, a board member of the La Jolla Art Association and member of P.S.W.C. as well as the Degas Pastel Society, is a recognized artist who has artwork in North America as well as in Europe. She says inspirational scenes in Baja California such as the San Pedro Mártir Mountains, the Pacific Ocean, and Indian tribes offer valuable tools of inspiration for her artwork. Contact her representative in the States by writing to: Elvia Tadeo, PO Box 2229, Vista, CA 92085.

Where shall I shop for Mexican gifts?

Las Flores Bazar, located on Blvd Benito Juarez 1560 across from the Hotel Quintas Del Mar, has many lovely items that would make unique gifts. Everything from Mexican dresses to rustic outdoor furniture is offered for sale. Jesus and Alicia Navarro Valdez will greet you and become your friends. Tell them, "Roberta sent me."

Mario's at Puerto Nuevo is the second booth on the right after entering through the arch in Puerto Nuevo. Unique artwork, jewelry and pottery of the finest taste are offered at reasonable prices. Mario will treat you as a good friend as you select your purchases.

Another gift store is called **Casa de Four Seasons**. All occasion florals, gifts, cards, furniture, event planning, ribbon, etc. are offered, with designers on staff. They have custom holiday décor for homes, restaurants, and shopping centers. Located at 58 Calle de la Palma, Rosarito, B.C., they're open from 10AM to 6PM daily except on Wednesday. Phone: (011-52-661) 31494.

Tijuana Arts and Crafts Center—40 artisan factory stores offer the largest selection of fine handcrafted arts including such items as: Talavera, pewter, silver, iron, ceramic, blown glass, textiles, marble and granite fountains. Located on the corner of Revolucion and 7th, next to Jai Alai. Phone (011-52-66) 38-4737 – E-mail: bazarmex@telnor.net

Where can I find Mexican jumping beans?

Mexican jumping beans can be found in most of the Rosarito and Tijuana gift stores in August and September. They are seasonal little brown beans that move around because worms are trying to get out of the pod to become a moth. It's fun to have them race one another off a tabletop. Patience is required.

Where is it safe to purchase jewelry?

Street merchants offer jewelry at bargain prices. They may represent their goods to be real silver but most likely they are not.

Casa Rosales, located across from Quinta Del Mar, offers a wide assortment of quality jewelry. You can have confidence that every piece in the store is made of the finest materials. George Rosales, owner, is a knowledgeable jeweler who will work with you to design anything you desire. Many customers will take personal jewelry to him to redesign. For instance, an inherited or pre-divorce wedding set with a lovely diamond can be melted down and fashioned into a lovely slide to be worn on a flat chain around the neck. Loose stones can be made into earrings, rings or a necklace. Let your imagination turn old pieces into new. George will help you fashion the jewelry of your dreams at practical prices. Custom design gold and silver, gem cutting and jewelry repair are offered. Call (011)(52)(66) 12-02-12. 194 & 294 Ave. Juarez, Rosarito, B.C.

Inges Jewelry offers reasonably priced, uniquely designed silver jewelry. Armando Ortega is the owner. His shop is located in the *mercado* behind El Nido Restaurant off the main street in Rosarito. Ave. Juarez #306 Suite J-15-18. Call (011-52-661)-220-93.

Where can I find high-quality stained glass?

Stained glass is very easy to find in Baja California. The quality and color differs greatly but the prices are all reasonable. **Tiffany Collections** in Tijuana offers original as well as custom items that are the best available. Tiffany lampshades, stained glass, beveled glass, blown glass, sun catchers and Christmas ornaments are sold here. Located through an alley and downstairs in Pasaje Comercial Revolucion 942, local 105, Revolucion Ave. between 3rd & 4th Streets, it offers a wide selection of high quality goods. Call (011-52-66)-85-06-94.

Where can I buy kitchen items?

A restaurant supplies stores called **Solomon Berger** sells professional-quality kitchen items. Everything from pots and pans to stainless steel silverware is sold. Located on Av. Negrete 1431-4, in Tijuana, the phone number is (011-52-66) 84-79-10.

Where can I purchase outdoor cement stepping stones, figurines, fountains or tables?

On the *Libre* or free road at K-40 is a place called **Curios Las Gaviotas** where the pieces are well made and reasonably priced. Call Agustin Diaz at (661) 41075.

Are there florists in town?

Yes. South of town at **La Misión**, where the free road separates from the pay road, there is a nursery that offers flowers for a reasonable price to those who venture out on Friday afternoons. They ship flowers to the States and sell their excess for bargain prices to local residents at the end of the week.

If you can't travel out of Rosarito for the bargain, then go visit the lady who is located on the side street just behind and to the left of the Derby Restaurant. Her prices are bargains compared to anything in the States. Just think, at $5, a fresh arrangement could be purchased each day!

The Mexican florists know how to make the most beautiful bouquets. Just visit any of many florist shops on main street.

Where can I order custom-made furniture?

Just tell Belinda and Jose what you want or bring in a picture and it will be professionally created for you at **Casa Bonita** in downtown Rosarito, on the main street, Benito Juarez, at the corner of Lazaro Cardenas. Check out their showroom for tasteful ready-made items. A computer table within a cabinet with doors is a great idea for those who want to close off their mess or keep the computer behind lock and key. They also offer pottery and hand-blown glassware. Call (011-52-661) 3-0209.

Is there an upholstery shop in Rosarito?

Yes. Tapiceria Sinaloa is located at the north end of town at K-21.5. Rene Castro, the proprietor, says, "All work guaranteed. We use American materials." Just bring your sofa, chair or whatever and he will complete the job to your satisfaction. A customer named Aurora says:

> I brought two chairs and an ottoman on Sunday to be re-upholstered. By Thursday they were all completed for $196. The fabric was from drapes I found at a thrift store in the States. You should see how cleverly they matched the chairs with the fabric! I'm quite pleased!

Where can I order carpet and verticals?

Rangel & Associates, located one block south of Dragon Del Mar, offers great professional carpet installation and offers new carpets at reasonable prices. Ask for Antonio Rangel, owner. Telephone: (011-52-661) 2-1426.

What carpet or upholstery cleaning service should I use?

Express truck-mounted steam cleaning does an excellent job. Call Alvazo Villaloa at (011-52-661) 21911 in Rosarito or (619) 904-3879 in San Diego.

Where can I find adequate home maintenance service?

Adolfo Kim offers help for any type of repair in Rosarito. His local phone number is 66-49-94-16. He's very reliable and will keep his appointments. His satisfied clients say:

> I don't hesitate to recommend Adolfo to do work in your home. He found a leak in my pipe that no one else could identify. He dug five feet under my place to locate and fix it and then made it accessible in case another leak ever occurs. He rates as the best!

> Adolfo came when he said he would to replace old carpets with new tile that matched the tile already there. I tried for eight months to get someone else to do the work but they never came. Adolfo can be trusted to do what he says he will do.

My place looks clean and tidy now that Adolfo has painted it inside and outside. He did a very professional job. I'm pleased with his work.

Is there an appliance repair service available?

Call **Servicio Muños** at (661) 2278 in Rosarito for appliance repair work. You'll be pleased!

Sam Kaplan is reliable and knowledgeable. Call 2-0595 to make an appointment for Rosarito. Leave a message on his recorder and he'll call back when he has a chance.

Is it possible to get television satellite service?

Television reception can be troublesome without a satellite; the entire world is available with a good satellite system. Residential and commercial service is offered by **American Satellite**. Ask for Rich Wickern at 91-661-4-1422. Pick out the latest satellite and bring choice into your life.

Are there laundromats available in Rosarito?

Yes. The word for laundromat in Spanish is *lavamatica*. One is located at the north end of town in the Quinta Plaza shopping center, while another is located between Calle Acacias and Calle Roble on the east side of the main road.

Some subdivisions have machines available for those who reside there. Try the **San Antonio Del Mar** laundromat located behind the mini mart. It costs 75¢ per load. There are only two machines, but it's available for public use because it's located outside the security gate.

Does Rosarito have a good body shop for repairs on my car?

Yes. There's an excellent body shop in downtown Rosarito. It's called **James Body Shop** located on a street behind the main street at Jose Ma Morelos #30 Col. Echeverria, Rosarito, B.C., Mexico. Call 2-16-60. He paints, does bodywork, welds and does artwork on cars. If you have a car that needs work, give it a try. His workmanship is exquisite and affordable.

Is there a local mini storage in Rosarito?

Yes. It's located on the *Libre* road south of town at Ma William's Trailer Park. It's adequately secured and costs $60 per month.

Baja Malibu RV & Bodega Storage is located across the Cuota from the Oasis Hotel just North of Rosarito. It's fenced and lighted for security.

What companies offer transportation of household goods or other goods into or out of Mexico?

Alberto Jaramillo Jr.—Call for free estimate if you're planning to live in Mexico and you would like to bring your furniture. International moving from Mexico to the United States and from the United States to Mexico is totally covered by insurance. For a free estimate, call (011-52-661) 35059 or (706) 612-1342.

A resident of Bajamar testifies:

> I had this company move my household furniture down to Mexico where I live now. They took care of everything from the packing in the United States to the unpacking in Mexico. Everything was done professionally at a reasonable price. Nothing was broken or lost. I can recommend them highly to others.

What do I do when I need my propane tank refilled?

Propane trucks make daily routine runs. If you need a refill, just hang out a red flag and the truck will stop to refill your tank. Certain subdivisions have set delivery days. For instance, San Antonio del Mar's day is Thursday, while Las Gaviotas is Wednesday. Other projects such as Club Marena handle refills through the office, not bothering the individual homeowners with it.

Caution: Check your tank for leaks periodically. Corrosion is a problem in the moist salt air and old tanks need to be carefully monitored. Propane is highly flammable and must be properly sealed.

Note: The red flag is used in Rosarito, not necessarily in other towns.

I understand I can't mail payment of utility bills. What do I do?

You may go into each utility company to pay for the bill in person, but you should be prepared for a long wait because others are also making payments. You could purchase a residence such as a condominium where the electric, propane and water are paid in common so the association makes the payment, or you could pay for a service to care for your payments. **The Insurance and Utility Management Company** located at the Quinta Plaza Center in Rosarito offers such service. Phone (011-52-661) 21295 or E-mail: cuadros@telnor.net. They will set up an account to pay the following: electricity, water, propane, telephone, property taxes, bank trust, weekly maid fee, etc.

Where can I get a good massage?

Many hotels offer massages, but if you desire to have an expert masseuse come to your home, give **Irma** a call. Her telephone number is 66-308-242. She offers a minimum of three hours for $90. Facial massages are as relaxing as full body massages. She brings her own folding massage table and all the lotions with her. Don't expect her to come at the last minute. This lady is busy and must be booked ahead of time.

Esther gives a wonderful massage at **Don Ami Salon**, located next to the El Nido Restaurant. Call (011-52 661)-2-0066 for an appointment. You'll be delighted with the reasonable cost.

Casa Playa at the Rosarito Hotel offers European-style

spas, hydrotherapy baths, facials, herbal wraps and messages. Call (011-52-661) 2-26-87 or (619) 498-8230. Internet address: http://www.rosaritohtl.com

Are mineral baths offered locally?

Yes. **Aguas Termales Valparaiso** in Tijuana on Avenida de La Paz offers mineral baths, mud wraps, facials and full body massages for a total of $60 for all. Call (011-52- 66) 24-07-86 for appointments.

Is a beauty salon available?

There are salons at the hotels that are adequate, but the prices and quality of service are professional at **D'Lupita's**, across from the Las Brisas Hotel. Men's and ladies' styling, cuts, pedicures and manicures are offered. Phone (011-52-661) 2-2583 for appointments, although drop-ins are welcome. Check it out. French tip polish application is only $2.

MONEY MATTERS

It's good to have money and the things that
money can buy, but it's good too, to check up
once in a while and make sure you haven't
lost the things that money can't buy.
—George Horace Lorimer

Too many people forget that the supreme
duty of every man is to make a life,
since almost anyone can make a living.
—R. Roy Keaton

What is the cost of living in Baja California, Mexico?

Property taxes may be at a high of $150 per year while

electricity and gas are $10 per month each. It costs $2 to get fingernails polished, $11 for fingernail tips and $4 for a man's haircut. A great meal can be purchased for $3.95. Why bother to cook? The following anecdotes are from my journal:

Today I had lunch at El Tios Restaurant in Rosarito. The owner and waiters greeted me as an old friend even though I've only eaten there three or four times since my friend Adolfo Kim introduced me to this wonderful, humble place, located on a side street across from the PeMex gas station in the center of Rosarito. It seems like all the local Mexicans enjoy the home cooking. They don't care about "ambiance." The fans in the ceiling rotate slowly. The drinks in large glass jugs await the next ladle to dip, and the tortilla cook stands by the hot grill to produce a fresh bundle of the hot flour flat bread or the famous gorditas, plump and full of deliciously spiced pork, beef or chicken. Two gorditas cost $1.40 and believe me, they're nothing like those tasteless gorditas at Taco Bell. Today I ordered fish, rice, beans, salad and a Fanta strawberry drink which cost 28 pesos or about $3.50 total.

Yesterday I visited the Sunday flea market just off the main street of Rosarito. It was teaming with people of all ages looking for bargains in the makeshift stands that lined the street. Everything from sunglasses to makeup to car parts was being sold. My favorite was the food that's sold by the farmers. I stopped at a vegetable stand where I grabbed a tub and tong to make my selection of bananas, avocados, onions and cantaloupes. When my tub was full, I was charged 14 pesos, a little less than $2. That's my vegetable budget for the entire week.

The cost of a cleaning lady for eight hours is no more than $20 a day.

Real estate prices are reasonable too. $300,000 can buy a big *hacienda*, while a normal house with no ocean view can be found for $90,000. Lots with a view go for a low of $18,000 to a high of $90,000. Construction is going for a high of $50 a square foot—that's for the best builder-architect available.

It's possible to live nicely on less than $1000 a month for basics, especially if no outstanding debt exists. Traveling and purchasing fancy items would require more, naturally. It's obvious that Social Security, pension or other resources definitely offer added value in Mexico especially when the dollar to peso fluctuates to favor the dollar.

Note: There is a difference between tourist prices and local prices. Most locals learn quickly where to find bargains.

Do I need to convert US dollars into pesos?

It is wise to have some pesos on hand for certain services but in tourist establishments in Tijuana, Rosarito and Ensenada dollars are used regularly. However, there are certain places that will quote prices only in pesos. In these cases, beware of on-the-spot conversions. For instance, a gas station may tell you the peso price. You give them dollars and they will give you change in pesos. Ask what change rate they use to calculate the exchange. The peso fluctuates in value so much that you may be losing money. The best plan is to have both pesos and dollars in your wallet. If you use pesos, then expect pesos in change. If you use dollars, expect dollars in change. In some cases, the person giving change will say they don't have change in dollars so they give it in pesos or not at all. In that case, it's obvious that pesos should have been used. I like to use pesos in grocery stores, gas stations and with local merchants who don't deal with tourists on a regular basis.

Where should I convert my dollars into pesos?

Banks offer the current conversion rates. However, they often have long lines and odd hours. In Rosarito and Tijuana there are 24-hour ATM machines that accept American bank cards and dispense pesos based on the current exchange rate. **Banamex** and **Bancomer Banks**, located on the main street, have ATM machines with locked access doors offering privacy during the transaction. Some department stores in Tijuana have ATM machines.

Are the exchange houses fair in changing money?

These places, called *casas de cambio* are located in California USA border towns and on downtown streets of Northern Baja California cities. The exchange rates are posted with *vente*, meaning "sell" and *compra*, meaning "buy" prices. The number following *vente* is the amount you get per dollar when you sell back pesos for dollars. The number following the word *compra* is how much you get when you buy pesos per dollar. Be certain to count the pesos you are given and ask questions. Find out how much they take out for commissions for making the exchange. If time isn't a concern, it would be wise to shop around for the best prices. It's surprising how they differ. A calculator may be a wise item to carry.

Will hotels change my money?

Yes, but check the cost of commission and rate. If it's a small out-of-the-way hotel, it may not provide the service. In fact, it may not even accept credit cards for payment.

Are credit cards and checks easy to use?

Credit cards and checks are not used as commonly as in the United States. Tourist establishments will accept credit cards, but the smaller, more local merchants don't have the banking ability to do so. Foreign checks aren't often accepted unless rapport is established with the merchant. It's difficult and in some cases expensive for the merchant to cash them. In recent years, many merchants have been the victims of fraudulent US checks, leaving them leery of foreigners. Ask about policy before service is rendered.

Note: A service charge from 6 to 10% may be added to the bill when a credit card is used. Be certain to read the bill before you sign or ask about the policy before you purchase.

Can I get a credit card from a Mexican bank?

Yes, but you must have proof of being in Mexico legally.

How do I determine the cost when two prices are listed on an item for sale?

One price, pesos, will have an **N$** in front of it or **m/n** after the price. M/n means *moneda national* or national money. It may have **$$** in front of it instead. The other price, dollars, will have **Dlls** or just one $ in front or behind it. There is no standard, so if in doubt, ask the merchant.

What types of accounts are offered in Mexican banks?

It is possible to choose between a peso-denominated checking account, or a US dollar account with proof of US citizenship. A minimum amount of $500 or $1,000 is required for regular or money market accounts, respectively.

What documentation do I need when I open a bank account?

◆ a **picture ID** such as a driver's license or passport

◆ **proof of address**, such as a bill or rental agreement

For more information, call Banamex at 01-800-021-3000 or 225-3000 from Mexico or find this site on the Internet: http://www.banamex.com.mx

Can I do on-line banking in Mexico?

Yes. Technology is starting to be used in Mexico. **Bitel Bank** is one of the largest financial holding companies in Mexico. In 1992 it was acquired by the government under the reprivatization process. It offers on-line services. See their website for more information: http://www.bital.com.mx or call (66) 88-19-14 to locate a local branch.

What is the proper manner in which to pay while in Mexico?

The Mexicans consider it rude when a person plops down or throws money at them. The proper way to pay is *mano a mano* or hand to hand. When you pay for something, hand the money to the recipient, looking him/her in the eye. Mutual respect results in a positive encounter. Say *gracias* or thank you.

How do I get a waiter to bring me the bill?

It is a polite custom in Mexican restaurants for the waiter to allow a customer to enjoy himself until he is ready to ask for the check. Never snap your fingers or get impatient because the check is not delivered to you without your request. When you're ready for it, you may catch the waiter's eye across the room and write in the air or on your hand but it is the custom, if the waiter is within hearing distance, to say, *"La cuenta, por favor,"* meaning, "the check, please."

When ordering a drink in a bar, do not set money on the table or bar as is the custom in the United States. Wait until you're finished and simply ask for the bill as described above. A tab is always started automatically upon ordering.

How much should I pay in tips?

Apply the same rules as in the United States. Ten to 15% of the bill is adequate in restaurants. Be certain to leave money in a tip jar for entertainers, especially when you request a certain song. Also, security guards in subdivisions often provide extra services such as helping to start a dead battery or directing traffic for a party. If they receive a tip, they will be happy to help next time. I also like to give them a can of Pepsi, cup of coffee or freshly baked cookies as an occasional treat as I pass through the guard gate.

Is there a difference in the way a local foreign resident is treated as opposed to a tourist?

Yes. Tourists may be charged more than a local, simply because they don't have a knowledge of local prices. For instance, when I pulled into a parking garage, I asked the attendant what it would cost for my car to be washed while it was parked. He quoted a higher price to me before I told him I lived here. It cost $3 for a hand-washed job for me. $5 or more can be charged for an unsuspecting tourist. The attendant is a wise enough businessman to know I'll return and will probably refer others to him, whereas a tourist is not likely to ever return.

Another time, while waiting in line to cross the border into the US, I asked a street vender how much a bag of candied nuts cost. At first his answer was $6. I laughed. When I told him I lived in Mexico, the price went down to 50¢.

Even if you retain use of an out-of-country license plate, a Red Cross decal on your car window indicates you're a local resident, since they are given to those who join the organization. Shopkeepers, other drivers and the police will treat you differently if they see the decal. (See page 225 for information on the Red Cross in Mexico.) For instance, when there's a road check, you may be motioned to move ahead, while a tourist may be delayed for inspection.

Consider joining **Footprinters** at René's Restaurant by talking to either Harry or Carl who are patrons after 6 PM. It is a group who helps the police to obtain needed items. In exchange for a donation to the Rosarito Police Department, you will receive a decal to post in your car indicating you have contributed to the police funds for new equipment etc. (See page 177 under government agencies for more information.)

What do I do when a beggar wants money?

Rosarito has few, if any, beggars. However, if one approaches, spare a few coins if you have available change. If you don't have anything to share, hold your index finger up and wave it back and forth. No words need be exchanged because they're familiar with that signal which their mother uses to say no.

At the US border when traveling north leaving Mexico, there is a sign written by a Mexican charity organization, **DIF** or **Sistema Para El Desarrollo Integral De La Familia**, that paraphrased states, "Don't give money to the beggars if you want to help them. You'll only keep them on the streets, instead of coming to us for help." DIF evidently teaches them to be self-sufficient. Kathy Wasson states:

> DIF is a charity organization I support by offering my time as a volunteer. The mayor's wife of each town is in charge of this charity, which offers lessons to poor people about cleanliness with the goal of aiding them

to become self-sufficient. We've bundled up clothes and food for them, but they have to take lessons in hygiene and sanitation in order to receive them. The first time I went up into the hills to help them with DIF, I cried to see such a pathetic state of poverty. My animals live better than they do. I'm only one person, so I'll do what I can through volunteering my services to this wonderful Mexican organization. If anyone wants to help with contributions of clothes, money or time, DIF knows just what is needed. Call (011-52-661) 3-00-80 for Rosarito DIF.

Beggars are more common in Tijuana because there are more tourists. It's the belief of many that they're mostly con artists who make a lot of money off the many naive tourists who feel sorry for them. In fact, some will "borrow" a baby for a day's "work" just to con the tourists into having empathy and offering more money on behalf of the "poor baby." Tijuana is a wealthy, vibrant city with a very low unemployment rate. If a person really wants a job, he will find it. Others say:

> I always give to the poor when I see them. Those who have lost limbs and are struggling to survive deserve my loose change.

> When the people in white ask for money, I always donate because they give me a blessing. It makes me feel good to give something to a good cause.

Do I have to pay taxes?

Contact the IRS for detailed information concerning the

requirements for every citizen to pay taxes. Just because you live outside of the United States, it doesn't mean your tax obligations are finished. Any Mexican citizen who works in the United States or receives income from the United States has an obligation to pay taxes as well. Call the American Embassy in Mexico City at (011-52-5) 209-9100 ext. 3557 for more information.

Can I do business in Mexico?

Yes. The Foreign Investment Law of 1993 and NAFTA, the North American Free Trade Act, have opened many doors in Mexico that were previously closed to foreigners. Mexico has legal requirements that are essential to understand and implement when setting up or conducting business. It is therefore advisable to operate under the advice of a knowledgeable Mexican lawyer and accountant who will coordinate to meet the necessary legal requirements with your best interests in mind. Mexico has strict registration, tax and labor laws, which need to be understood by those conducting business. These laws are not to be taken lightly. For instance, if necessary visas are not obtained, being shut down and sent home is a continual and unnecessary threat. If labor laws are broken, it could cause severe financial consequences. If an employee is fired, he most likely will have the right to sue for punitive damages as well as salary compensation. Remember, the government wants its citizens to be employed and it will protect their employment rights in court. There are only a few violations that will be accepted as justifiable reasons for dismissal and those must be addressed in writing and within a certain period of time. Just as in the United States, awareness and compliance with the laws will prevent unnecessary problems. Don't assume the laws are the same as in the States. They are not. Become aware and informed. The culture is different. The laws are different. Talk with other employers and find out what their experiences have been. Don't invest time or money without doing adequate research.

Don't get discouraged. Baja California is ripe and ready for business investments. It offers opportunity for those who have the foresight and desire to succeed. Pay a visit to this area. The economic signs of present and future growth are abundantly evident. (See page 320 for a further discussion.)

It's possible to obtain employment in U.S. embassies in Mexico. See the following Internet site for more information: http://www.usembassy.org.mx/eacsinfo.html.

Internet sites that offer further business information are the following:

http://www.amcham.com.mx
American Chamber/ Mexico's services

http://www.mexico-trade.com
Mexico Business Opportunity and Legal Framework

An audio-cassette series on doing business in Mexico can be ordered at (619) 479-3476. Ask for *Viva Mexico* six-hour audio-cassette series and work book. Credit cards accepted.

What television commercials are produced in Mexico?

Mexican commercials are highly creative and unusually entertaining. They can be quite different from those we see in the States.

The Mexican sense of humor and ability to market cleverly are shown in their television commercials. I'll describe two commercials that tickled my sense of humor. Picture a beautiful young girl who is descending stairs to get to the ground floor level of an apartment building. She leaves her apartment on an upper floor carrying a bottle of purified water. When she arrives on the bottom floor she slips through wrought iron security bars on the front door without unlocking it. When she's on the outside, she takes a sip of the water whose name on the bottle is shown clearly on the screen. A handsome man is on the inside holding the key in his hands as though he had wanted to open the door for her. She smiles at him but waves and turns away to walk down the street. End of commercial. Was the message that she was thin enough to slip through the bars because she drank the water?

Another commercial ended with a surprise product. I don't think this one would ever be aired in the United States. Envision two beautiful young women arriving on a bridge in a convertible. Two handsome young men are paddling a kayak toward the underside of the bridge on a river that runs underneath the girls' location. The two females get out of the car, lean over the side of the bridge and then one of them drops something over the side toward the young men in the kayak. The next shot is not of the men catching something. Instead, it shows them in a river without water.

They're stuck on riverbed rocks in their kayak. What did the girls throw into the water? The most absorbent maxi pad ever made!

You don't even need to know how to speak Spanish to catch the message of these commercials. Anyone who thinks the marketing power of these companies is lacking should watch these clips on television.

What can happen to me if I work in Mexico without proper Mexican papers?

Mexican immigration officials posing as patrons will visit business establishments to catch violators who work without proper documentation. One man who went into a retail establishment to fix electrical wiring was asked to produce his documentation that allowed him to work. He didn't have it. As a result, his car was confiscated and he was deported back into the United States on the spot. (See page 198 for more information.)

What is a maquiladora?

A *maquiladora* is a factory originating from the United States but operating in Mexico. It obtains cheap labor for its production as a foreign assembly plant while providing jobs to Mexican nationals. Electrical, textile, jewelry and other factories import raw materials duty free and export finished products. Tariffs are charged only on value added as the goods return to the United States. The finished product does not remain in Mexico. Many such factories exist in Baja California benefiting both Mexicans and

Americans. In the early 1900s, Sony became the first *maquiladora* to operate in Tijuana; now 900 *maquiladoras* operate there. A manufacturing company will come into Mexico with its managers and technical specialists to set up a plant. They train Mexican managers and technicians who will, after four or five years, run the plant without the US counterparts who return to their country of origin. Mexican production in this way has become competitive to other manufacturing countries.

Chevy, Volkswagen, or Sony are names that are familiar to most people. The quality found in Mexican production is not to be disparaged. In fact, if you have a Sony television in your house right now, it was probably manufactured in Tijuana! For information about labor relations for *maquiladoras* see this Internet site: http://www.desistemas.com/labormex

CHAPTER EIGHT

SPANISH LANGUAGE

Sometimes, familiarity and comfort
need to be challenged. There are times when
you must take a few extra chances and create
your own realities. Be strong enough to at least try to
make your life better. Be confident enough that you
won't settle for compromise just to get by . . . .
—Deanna Beisser

Do I need to know how to speak Spanish in order to live in Baja California?

Generally the answer is no, because so many local residents know English, especially those people who work in the tourist sector. However, there are many local residents who only speak Spanish. After all, it's the official language of Mexico. There are many instances when speaking Spanish can be a practical asset. Communicating needs to delivery-men or repairmen could be frustrating without the ability to speak Spanish. Also, recorded Spanish telephone messages could be impossible to interpret. If you're a tourist or if you want to be like Americans who live here for 20 years without learning Spanish, you can get by, but you'll either be dependent on others to occasionally translate or you'll have moments of frustration. You'll miss the nuances and passion of the colorful Mexican culture. You'll always be an outsider but perhaps you won't care. Maybe you want to hang out only with other Americans. The advantage of living in Rosarito is that you have a choice. The choice is yours to make.

An anecdote illustrating how a little knowledge can lead to misunderstanding is quoted from Raul's Restaurant's newsletter:

> Using the language is important, but watch the usage. A customer asked a waiter *cuantos* when ordering a chili rellenos plate and was told *tres*. He was upset when the bill was $7.75, not $3.00. He had asked "how many" when saying *cuantos*. "How much" should have been *cuanto*. When in doubt avoid Spanish and use English.

I disagree with the idea that he should have used English. The person paid a small price for a lesson he will never repeat. Hopefully, he improved his knowledge and will never make the same mistake again. He may be out a few dollars, but he enriched his knowledge of the Spanish language in a way that won't easily be forgotten.

Generally, Mexicans enjoy my attempts at speaking Spanish. They take time to correct me when I make errors. Someday I will speak Spanish fluently. In the meantime, I will learn *poco a poco* or "little by little".

However, before speaking, I will ask if a person understands English, because it sometimes can be demeaning and an annoyance if I assume they don't speak English and I take their time with my faltering Spanish. I've learned to discern between those who are willing to help and those who don't want to be bothered.

Are there Spanish words I already know?

Yes. There are many Spanish words that are the same as English words. A creative approach to learning Spanish is in a lesson book entitled *Madrigal's Magic Key to Spanish* by Margarita Madrigal, published by Doubleday. In the Preface she states that "It is the essence of this method to make learning Spanish a pleasure for you." She starts her book with illustrations of words that are the same in both languages. Each chapter ends with a chart to summarize the lesson. This chart, on page 13, refers to the endings of the words:

    I. OR (identical)
      el doctor
    II. AL (identical)
      el animal
      personal
    III. BLE (identical)
      el cable
      probable

IV. IC=ICO
  el Atlantico
  electrico
V. ENT=ENTE
  ANT=ANTE
  el presidente
  excelente
  el restaurante

She recommends that her students write these words on cards so that when they have a quiet moment, they'll have them handy to study. These cards will help students progress twice as fast as they would without them. Buy the book. It holds many easy-to-learn lessons such as the one above.

How can I place the Spanish symbols on my computer if I don't have a special Spanish program?

Microsoft Word has a symbols option that lets you insert a letter with its diacritical mark. The symbols box is accessed through the insert bar. The following directions can be used also:

◆ To place an **acute** mark on the letter:
  Hold down the CTRL button
  Plus hold down the 'apostrophe button
  While typing the LETTER
  Á

◆ To place a *tilde* over a letter:
  Hold down the CTRL button
  Plus SHIFT button

Plus TILDE button ~
Let go
Then type the LETTER
Ñ

♦ To place a *diaeresis* over a letter:
Hold down the CTRL button
Plus SHIFT
Plus COLON
Plus the LETTER
Ä

♦ To place an **upside-down question mark**
at the beginning of a sentence:

Hold down the ALT button:
Plus the CTRL button
Plus the SHIFT button
Plus the question mark button ?
¿

♦ To place an **upside-down exclamation mark**
at the beginning of a sentence:
Hold down the ALT button
Plus the CTRL button
Push the SHIFT button
Plus the exclamation button
¡

What is the best way to learn to speak Spanish?

The best way to learn is practice, practice, practice. Allow
yourself to be exposed to it as much as possible. When we

asked people how they learned the English language, many said, "I watched American television constantly." Listening to Spanish-speaking radio stations and watching television or videos in Spanish will increase your knowledge. Speak what you know and listen carefully to corrections. It takes time but don't give up. Every mistake can be a lesson. I can't remember a word I hear once, but if I have an experience with it, I can recall it easily.

What is the standard greeting in Spanish?

In Spanish the greeting changes with the time of day. Try the following:

Buenos días is used in the mornings. It means **good morning**.
Buenas tardes is used after noon. It means **good afternoon**.
Buenas noches is used after sunset. It means **good night**.

When do I use *por favor*?

Anytime a request is made it is wise to use *por favor*, which means **please**. If someone says *"sientese, por favor"* they are asking you to **sit down, please**. Rules of politeness are used, especially when speaking to elders. *Ayudame, por favor* means **please help me**. I've found it a helpful expression to use many times as I get lost driving or when I'm confused about something.

What does *mande* mean?

It is an expression used in response to someone who has just said something to you that you want repeated. In

English we would say, "What?" or "Eh?" It's pronounced "Monday", but it has nothing to do with the day of the week.

What is the difference between the meaning of *picante* and *caliente*?

Each word means "hot" but *picante* is used to describe spicy hot while, *caliente* refers to temperature.

What is the proper way to say, *Thank you* and *You're welcome*?

Gracias means **thank you**, while *de nada* means **you're welcome**. Translated literally it means **it was nothing**. Those two words summarize the generous hospitality and loving nature of the Mexican people. They will graciously give help and then say, "It was nothing," when appreciation is shown.

What road signs written in Spanish should I learn?

Always carry a Spanish-English dictionary. Use it when you don't know the English translation of a sign. You will learn on the go a little at a time, but you'll be surprised at how proficient you will become.

Peligrosa means **dangerous**. If you see it on a road sign, it means the road is dangerous. If it's on a truck, it means the load is dangerous.

No tire basura means **don't litter**.

Abierto means **open** while *cerrado* means **closed**.

What is a *palapa*?

A *palapa* is an outdoor structure with a thatched roof much like a gazebo. It's often used for covered outdoor living.

Where can I go to learn how to speak Spanish?

There are instructors available who teach private or group lessons at a local level. Watch bulletin board announcements and newspaper ads for the names and phone numbers of those who teach. Adolfo Kim taught our group at Rene's Restaurant three times a week last season, but he is now doing construction work. He took us on field trips to Ensenada and Tijuana and taught us far more about the culture than just the language. Our group formed a warm bond with each other.

Is there a formal language training school available?

The Language College of Baja California in Ensenada has the following philosophy as stated on their Webpages:

> Our program was designed specifically to help students identify and eliminate barriers to speaking Spanish.

We realize that in large classes of 20-30, most students are not comfortable speaking a foreign language in front of their classmates. They typically become frustrated and study behind a barrier that prevents them from speaking freely. We know that memorizing vocabulary lists for chapter tests does not encourage Spanish speaking. It can be a long, excruciating process if one only studies Spanish a few hours per week while being bombarded constantly with non-Spanish messages (i.e. television, radio and human encounters).

In the Spanish immersion program we offer in the sunny Pacific Ocean port city of Ensenada, Baja California, Mexico, you will be exposed to Spanish all day and every day. Our classes have six or fewer students, which allows individual attention and plenty of opportunity to speak Spanish.

There are no textbooks or exams. We don't grade our students. Each student is well aware of their progress and the effort they are putting forth. Our students grade themselves on their ability to communicate in Spanish . . . We are committed to creating the perfect environment for you to quickly learn to communicate in Spanish.

How do I contact the Language College?

Telephone: (011-52) 61-74-56-88 or 909-945-3392
E-mail address: college@bajacal.com
URL address: http://www.bajacal.com/

What are the benefits of speaking Spanish?

A young American man speaking flawless Spanish was asked for papers by an immigration official who wanted to catch him illegally working without papers at a fair. He answered the official in fluent Spanish, explaining that he had lived in Mexico all his life. The official immediately apologized for bothering him and went to look for his American boss, hoping, I assume, to catch him working without papers. The official could have deported the offenders if they weren't working legally. In this case, the young man had no papers but his ability to speak Spanish led the official to think he was legally working. He had lived in Mexico since he was a little boy so his tongue was native.

Going through checkpoints where the army guards ask questions in Spanish offers little hassle if the driver speaks fluent Spanish. My friend Linda asked young men who carried machine guns questions about how long they were "stationed" there. They said they stay in little tents for a whole year at one location. Living in the middle of nowhere for a year would get boring for most young people. Each Mexican boy has to serve one year in the Mexican army, stationed at checkpoints in desolate areas. No wonder they enjoy chit-chatting with passers-by!

While in the local grocery store, I asked a stock boy where the vinegar was located. He didn't know English and I didn't know how to say it in Spanish, so I had to hunt down a bilingual person who gave me the correct word to use. It but cost me time, but now I'll never forget the Spanish word is *vinegre*. It's surprising how just adding one word each day helps build my vocabulary.

Although she never had trouble receiving the United States channels on TV, Kathy Wasson couldn't get the NFL Super Bowl game in English on her television set. It was only transmitted with Spanish-speaking announcers, so she had to watch the action without understanding the words of the sports commentators.

I had a hearty laugh when my friend spoke in halting Spanish with a thick English accent to a security guard who said in response, *"No hablo inglés,"* meaning **"I don't speak English."** Even speaking what we thought was Spanish didn't work with that particular guard!

C H A P T E R   N I N E

EDUCATION

They will tell you and encourage you to develop your
brain and your five senses. But that's only half of it;
that's only being half a human. The other half is to
develop the heart and the wits. . . . Never let anyone
rob you of your right to be complete. . . . Your brain
may fail you one day, but your heart won't.

—Fynn
Mr. God This Is Anna

How does the Mexican educational system differ from that of the United States?

Most Americans would be surprised to hear that Mexican
young people who transfer to a stateside school often find

themselves advanced by one or two grade levels. Why? The Mexican government has concentrated upon stressing the basic subjects such as math, science, reading and writing. They don't offer what they consider to be "after school extras" such as art or sports, which have to be privately arranged. Education is valued as a tool for improvement.

Mexican children are not required by the government to attend school past the sixth grade. The following is a breakdown of their schooling:

Jardín de Niños or **Garden of Children**—optional attendance for four to six year olds—equivalent to kindergarten.

Primaria or primary school—mandatory for ages six to 14 equivalent to grade school

Secundaria—high school equivalent—college prep courses

Secundaria-Technico—high school training for skilled technical fields

Colegio Technico—technical college for various studies

Universidad—university training for professional fields

Children are geared for a career when they reach junior high school. They then go to a prep or trade school depending upon their abilities and interests. Everything from auto mechanic schools to executive training and computer schools as well as full universities are available in Baja California. A look at the yellow pages reveals how serious the Mexicans are about education. Under escuelas or schools in the Tijuana phone book (also covers the Rosarito area) there are no less than twenty pages of schools listed.

What observations are made about the school children?

Heather Noonan says, "The children all look so clean and disciplined when they go to public school in their uniforms. No one is dressed any better than another so they must be able to better concentrate on their studies."

Children who live in areas where there are no schools have the opportunity to take classes on television. The government supports education enough to make this alternative possible.

> When I attended school in the United States after going to a Mexican school, I was advanced by one grade level. Now I'm back in the Mexican system. It's definitely more advanced in Mexico.
>
> —Rueben, 11 years old

Are private schools available?

There are choices of private schools that are excellent. When selecting a school, do proper research by visiting and getting recommendations from local residents. Linda Dobson who currently has a son in the eighth grade says, "I'm quite pleased with the education my son is receiving in Mexico. He's more advanced in the basics of science and math than his stateside contemporaries. He speaks both Spanish and English fluently and will have more choices in life than others as he decides his future."

Are there universities in Baja California?

Yes. There are four universities in Ensenada: **the University of Baja California**, **CICSE**, specializing in oceanography, **the National University of Mexico**, specializing in physics and astronomy, and **Cebates**. The **Universidad Autónoma de Baja California** also has locations in Tijuana and Mexicali. **El Colegio de La Frontera** has a campus overlooking the Pacific Ocean in Tijuana on the road to Rosarito. **The Universidad Iberoamericana** is located in Tijuana. Because Mexican universities are excellent in the science fields, United States universities such as Scripps and San Diego State join with them for research projects and exchange study in such programs as oceanography, geology and astronomy. (For an example, see Turtle Study on page 248.)

The National Observatory in the Sierra San Pedro Mártir National Park, which was constructed in consultation with astronomers of world renown, is one of the most advanced facilities in the world and it was built with great care. For example, the glass used for the instruments was imported from Germany. Scientists and university students from around the world visit this observatory to learn and to conduct research studies in conjunction with the Mexican universities. Many important discoveries have taken place at this observatory, located on the highest peak in Baja California, **El Diablo**. It is at least 10,000 feet above sea level. Take the dirt road turn-off on K-81 at **San Telmo de Abajo** to visit on Saturdays between 11 AM and 1 PM. It's 66 miles off the paved road on a rutted dirt grade. A high clearance, four-wheel-drive vehicle is necessary. Snow may be on the mountain in the winter months.

The Mexican government will train their employees with further educational courses at the universities. Many scientists who already have Masters degrees in their fields of expertise from various locations in Mexico, such as Sonora, Tabasco and Baja del Sur, met recently for advanced studies at the University of Baja California in Ensenada. They were traveling to the San Quintin oyster beds to do research when I met them. Their educational studies were to span a week's time in the classroom as well as in the field.

Is it expensive to send a child to a university in Mexico?

Linda Dobson says the following:

> At first I couldn't understand why I received blank expressions from my Mexican friends when I voiced concern about saving money for the upcoming four years of college education. Their lack of concern about finances finally made sense when I learned that college here in Mexico is available to students for the same amount of money I'm already paying for private school which is about $100 per month. No one feels money pressure as we do in the States because it just doesn't cost as much here in Mexico to send a child to the university. The education in some cases is far superior to that in the States. Everyone has the opportunity to go. For instance, my maid and her son lived in my guesthouse while he attended the university. She came to my door for a job one day telling me she was here with him so that he could attend the university. I hired her as my housekeeper and they both lived here until he graduated from college with an engineering degree. They

came here dirt poor with nothing, but now he will be able to support his family with his engineering abilities. The mother was so determined to give her son an education that she sacrificed her own time to support him. If I hadn't hired her, she would have persisted until someone else eventually hired her. In this way, the poor are given a chance for improvement.

Stan Gotlieb in his *Letters from Mexico*, which can be found on www.mexconnect.com, records examples of similar dedication in an article entitled, "A Tale of Two Students":

In Mexico, if you are poor, you can earn your higher education. A year as a teaching assistant is the price. The government provided room, board and a pitifully small stipend, and Pablo worked 10 hours a day, six days a week, teaching school in a town about four hours from his home. Now he is collecting his reward. The government absorbs his tuition but he must furnish his own books, some of which are quite expensive. He must also pay for his own rent, food, clothing and transportation. Therefore, he must work. . . . Pablo has a friend named Arturo. Arturo must pay all his tuition but receives a discount based on his grades. Since he maintains an average of 85%, he only has to pay half of his tuition (about 180 pesos—$55 at the time—per semester). If he could break 90%, schooling would be free . . . . *"Family"* is the strongest of the ties that bind Arturo, followed by *"God"* and *"Country."* When Arturo first came to the city, it was another cousin who arranged for living quarters for him. Shortly after his arrival, his father (Roberto) moved to town with Arturo's younger brother, Jorge (about 11 years old). His mother died of an infection after giving birth to Jorge. They came to be with Arturo.

Roberto understood that being so far from his family would be a very sorrowful experience for Arturo. It never occurred to Roberto that he needed to keep an eye on Arturo lest he fall into evil ways in the big city; nor was it necessary. He came because he believes that families are supposed to stay together . . . . Roberto has taken over part of Arturo's job in the market . . . . I asked Roberto how he was adjusting to all the changes. He told me that he preferred to live in the country, but that where one lives is a minor consideration compared to how one lives. "We are together, and we watch out for one another. That's what counts."

Note: To order Stan Gotlieb's E-mail newsletter, which describes life in Oaxaca, Mexico, access this website: http://www.dreamagic.com/stan/letters.html

It is this interest in education and the application of it by the next generation that offers hope for Mexico's future.

What is the attitude of the children in school?

Graham Mackintosh states the following in *Into a Desert Place*:

Apart from the cold store the school was the best-built building in camp. The walls were hung with colourful posters celebrating the great events and personalities of Mexican history. Suitably inspired I asked the class of sixteen youngsters to sing their national anthem. At first they reacted with shy smiles and giggles but with just a little prompting from Guillermo they were happy to oblige. I taped the performance. There was something about these children that was totally different from their British and American counterparts. They displayed a healthy and relaxed respect for themselves and for others that was quite refreshing. I wondered whether this was partly because they hadn't been subjected to the insidious daily dose of media violence, rebellion, anxiety and neurosis so prevalent in the privileged countries of the West.

Note: The above book may be purchased through W.W. Norton in paperback for $15.95. I highly recommend it.

The following observations were made when I traveled through the little town of El Rosario:

The road was blocked by a parade of students who marched down the street to the little green school house where they presented an outdoor program which honored their beloved country of Mexico. Each class wore matching outfits and marched in unison while one or two lucky students carried flags. One class of 12-year-old girls had four standard bearers who had taken the time to braid their hair into identical hairdos so they looked like quadruplets in their matching uniforms. Even the little first graders joined the parade in their little plaid skirts and red sweaters. It was Flag Day and they were celebrating their national respect for Mexico. The discipline and concentration of each child was remarkable. No one was out of step or goofing around, not even the five-year-olds. As they smiled when I took pictures as they marched along in the middle of the road, I wondered if they would be as happily dignified if they attended a school in my country of origin.

Linda Dobson adds insight into the compassion of the students in her son's school:

> When Hurricane Mitch caused a lot of damage in Central America, my son's eighth grade class was so upset about the suffering of the people, they decided to help those who lost their homes by collecting and earning over $15,000 to donate to the cause. The satisfaction they received from their efforts added to their own self-respect. They knew they had the ability to contribute effectively.

CHAPTER TEN

GOVERNMENT AGENCIES

Bandera de Mexico *Juramente a la Bandera*	**Flag of Mexico** **Oath to the Flag**
Bandera de Mexico	Flag of Mexico
Legado de Nuestros Heroes	Legacy of our Heroes
Sumbole de la unidad	Symbol of the Unity
De Nuestros Padres	Of our Fathers
Y de nuestros hermanos	And of our brothers
Te prometemos	We promise
Ser siempre fieles	To be always faithful
A los principios de libertad	To the principles of liberty
Y de justicia	And of justice
Que hacen de nuestra Patria	That makes our native land

La Nacion independiente	The independent nation
Humana y generosa	Humane and generous
A la que entregamos	To the commitment
Nuestra existencia	Of our existence.
	—Martin Barron Escamilla
	Guia Histoica de Baja
	California

Does Mexico have an agency in place to assist foreigners in their country?

Yes. Baja California offers help for visitors because its economy relies upon the tourist trade. The Secretary of Tourism says, "In Baja California, the private and public sectors have joined forces to offer our visitors a safe, enjoyable stay and to welcome them back."

What are the duties of the Mexican tourist assistance office?

A visitor is provided with general information and assistance as well as legal orientation free of charge.

Telephone Numbers:
Services of Secretary of Tourism are free of charge.

- ◆ Tijuana (66) 88 05 55

- ◆ Mexicali (65) 55 49 50

- ◆ Tecate (665) 4 10 95

- ◆ Ensenada(61) 7 2 30 22

- Rosarito (661) 2 02 00

- San Felipe (657) 7 11 55

- Vicente Guerrero (616) 6 22 16

- San Quintin (616) 6 24 98

- Algodones (653) 7 76 35

"The visitor will be represented by members of the Office for Tourist Assistance when he/she submits a written complaint about an irregularity in dealing with a provider of tourist services. When the visitor is unable to appear personally, this office will represent the visitor under a written authorization to do so."

If translation services are required or a Consulate who has jurisdiction in the state of Baja California needs to be contacted concerning a conflict, the tourist office will help.

It will intervene to investigate possible irregularities committed by those offering tourist or public services, if visitors need assistance at detention centers or emergency medical facilities, and when a visitor who has committed a misdemeanor is being held by authorities and encountering difficulties gaining release. It will also assist when a tourist is being held by the District Attorney's Office because of an accident or a minor infraction of the penal code.

What rights do visitors have in Mexico?

Article 17III
No individual can be detained or imprisoned for a civil debt.

Article 19III

While in detention no individual shall be subject to physical abuse or intimidation.

Article 20V

Persons detained may offer any proof necessary or required on behalf of their defense.

Article 20IX

An attorney may be appointed at the moment of detention.

When the defendant doesn't speak Spanish, the District Attorney will appoint an interpreter.

When the person being held is injured, he/she will be provided with medical attention in a public hospital or, in special circumstances, at a private facility under the supervision of the proper authorities.

The person being detained can obtain provisional release from the District Attorney by awarding a surety bond, provided that the case involves a traffic accident or is within the nature of a negligence crime violation, or the detainee was not under the influence of alcohol or drugs at the time of the accident, and that payment of damages is guaranteed.

For their part, tourists have the obligation to obey and respect all laws, authorities and government institutions.

The above information is from the *Tourist Assistance Guide* published by the Secretary of Tourism of Baja California. Call (011-52-66) 88-05-55.

What are the phone numbers
of the nearest consulates?

If you need assistance, don't hesitate to call the consul in Tijuana. You have rights as a foreign citizen that will be upheld by your consul in Mexico.

Tijuana Consulates:

(66) 81-74-00
or for emergencies call 619-692-2650—United States
(66) 84-0461—Canadian
(66) 88-26-63—Italian
(66) 85-45-02—Swedish
(66) 86-57-80—Spanish
(66) 80-18-30—German

What are the phone numbers of important
Mexican government agencies?

Rosarito (661)	Tijuana (66)	Ensenada (61)
Customs: 74-08-97	82-34-39	74-08-97
Immigration: 3-02-34	82-49-47	74-01-64
Green Angels: 2-11-44	80-10-40	_____

Should I be fearful of the Mexican police?

Mexico is a civilized country that has laws. The government hires the police to enforce the laws of the land. If you break the laws, the police will come after you. If you are stopped by the police while driving, stay calm. They will not hurt you. Being knowledgeable about Mexican laws and procedures is the key to handling an unpleasant situation.

How do I recognize valid police officers?

There are different types of Mexican police:

• **Municipal Police**—These are the local city police who provide surveillance, prevent crime and assist citizens. They take initial reports and can make arrests but they don't investigate crimes. They are in blue and white cars in Rosarito and on motorcycles in Tijuana. They wear uniforms. If they stop you and say they want to take you to the station so you can pay the fine, the best thing to do is to tell them you'll go with them. They may ask to see your driver's license and vehicle registration, but nothing else (not your passport or proof of citizenship). They should offer you a bilingual traffic ticket that states the amount of the fine for the specific violation and explains where to send it. There are four categories with the fines listed on the back:
A-$60—maximum fine
B-$40
C-$20
D-$12—minimum fine

The ticket will show the date and location of the offense. You have the option of going to the station to pay it or paying by mail.

• **State Judicial Police**—also called State Ministerial Police. They are plainclothes investigative agents who carry out arrest warrants and drive unmarked cars. They deal with serious crimes and work out of the State Attorney

General's office. You'll probably never see these police.

♦ **Federal Highway Police**—These are police who monitor traffic and proper vehicle registrations on the Federal Highways, much like the California Highway Patrol. They supervise ports and railroad areas as well. They can issue driving citations. They are Federal uniformed police officers who drive black and white cars.

♦ **Judicial Federal Police**—These are police officers from the Federal Attorney General's Office who investigate crimes against the Federal codes such as narcotics, firearms and money laundering. They operate check points on Mexican roads to search for drugs or weapons. These officials are not uniformed.

♦ **Mexican army officials**—They currently will perform checkpoint duty for the Federal Attorney General's office. They do have military weapons and have the authority to detain offenders. They can stop and search any vehicle at any time.

What do I do at road checkpoints?

DO NOT PANIC IF YOU'RE STOPPED AT A ROAD-BLOCK. You may be asked for your tourist permit if you are south of Ensenada, but most likely they'll just want to make certain you have no firearms or drugs in your vehicle. Always be polite and accommodating.

How do I recognize the Mexican Border Police?

♦ **Public Treasury Police**—These police are found at the border in royal blue Dodge Ram pickup trucks. They are in charge of verifying the legal entrance of declared items and vehicles crossing the border into Mexico. If you fail to stop when the red light flashes, they'll come after you in their trucks.

Are Security guards official policemen?

♦ **Security Guards**—Guards are on duty as security guards in different neighborhoods. The homeowner's associations of the various areas generally hire them. Some may be official off-duty policemen, others not. They are there to prevent trespassers from gaining entrance into the area and to see that neighborhood rules are enforced.

What do I do if they want a bribe?

If they are expecting a *mordida* or bribe the last place they want to go is to the station. Look at their vehicle for their unit number; get their badge number, and the officers' names. Don't confront them. Just keep your mouth shut. Either follow them to the station or ask them for your ticket to mail in the payment. You can turn them in later to their superiors who claim they'll fire such officers because they want to "clean up the problem."

According to the Secretary of Tourism, the following should be recorded to file a complaint:

♦ officer's name and badge number

♦ affiliation department

♦ time and place of the ticket

♦ officer's uniform color

♦ time of your detainment

Be aware that if you pay them off with a *mordida* it should not be more than $10 and it shouldn't be direct because it is illegal and you could end up in jail. Many Americans get ripped off this way. It will only stop when awareness and knowledge supersedes intimidation and lack of knowledge. Indulging in the practice of bribery will only perpetuate the problem.

What is the *Footprinters* organization?

It is an international organization that supports local police departments by donating needed equipment or supplies to them. Recently the Rosarito police received bulletproof vests and cages for their cars from this group of benefactors. The group was originally intended to include only people who were in the law enforcement business to promote closer cooperation between all agencies. Now it is open to anyone who is sympathetic to good law enforcement and its problems and has chapters in all cities and countries. Helping children be good citizens and catching the "bad guys" are important goals of this organization. If you become a member, you will receive an identification decal that will be instantly recognized by the police anywhere, especially by the Mexican police who are appreciative of their benefactors. To obtain more information about joining this group, contact Dr. Harry Ozaroski who can often be found at René's Cantina at the south end of Rosarito or call him at (619) 690-0773. His business card reads, *"Our purpose is to encourage friendship and cooperation between peace officers and all persons having a*

positive attitude towards preserving the public welfare."
His website address is:
http://www.mscomm.com/~footprint/
E-mail: DRHARRYO@CERAMA-TECH-INT.COM

Could you recount positive experiences foreigners have had with Mexican police?

Dick Warren describes the following incident:

> When I visited Tijuana as a young man I went into a bar only to be hustled by a woman who stole my wallet. After leaving the bar feeling the distress of losing all my money, I found a kindly policeman who asked me how much had been stolen. When I told him the amount, he said, "Wait right here. Don't go away." He then disappeared into the bar, returning in five minutes with my wallet in hand. As I counted the correct amount of money, he said, "I apologize, sir, for the inconvenience. We don't tolerate this type of theft against tourists. We want you to enjoy your time in Tijuana and to return here often."

Aurora adds another anecdote:

> When my daughter and I drove to Tijuana in order to shop, I carelessly made a "dumb-blonde" mistake in my driving. I looked into my rear view mirror and sure enough, there was a flashing red light coming after me. I stopped. The policemen who were young men wearing dark sunglasses got out of their car with frowns on their faces. One said to me, "Do you know you just caused an accident back there?" I answered in my most

distressed voice, "Oh, my goodness. Let me see what I've done."

"No. You don't have to go back there."

"Oh, but if I caused an accident, I must see what damage I caused."

"Well, er . . . they've already pulled away."

"But how will I know what I've done?"

"Well, it wasn't really so bad. We're going to have to take you to the station though."

I clutched my heart and said, "Oh, I have to go to the doctor's. I'm not well. I can't go to the station. You know, we're a mother and daughter here in your country as tourists. Why are you causing us so much stress? You should be ashamed of yourselves. You should be aiding us in finding our destination rather than causing us frustration. After all, we're guests in your country. Would you help us find our destination? Please?" They looked at each other, obviously not knowing what to do with this stressed-out woman and then shrugged their shoulders.

"All right. Just follow us. We'll lead you to where you want to go."

As we followed the police car as it guided us through the streets of Tijuana, my daughter who had missed the verbal interchange because she had stayed in the car, asked, "Mom, how did you do it?"

I answered with a grin, "I knew they had mothers so I just played the distressed mother role. It worked."

The above incident is a true account of how we obtained our personal police guides in Tijuana that day.

The police in Mexico are accused of cannibalizing cars for their parts or of keeping stolen vehicles for themselves. I've seen hundreds of unclaimed cars behind fenced, locked gates that belong to the police and wondered why they haven't been returned to their registered owners. The following incident illustrates that the police do, indeed, look for the owners:

> Our car was stolen from a California city in which we live. We thought we'd never see it again, but after six months we received a phone call from an Ensenada policeman. He said he had found our car in an Ensenada parking lot.
>
> We drove down to claim it and, sure enough, it was the car we had lost so many months before! We thought it was gone for good but, thanks to the Ensenada policeman, we have it back!

The following incident occurred because two people were in the wrong place at the wrong time and one was in the right place at the right time:

> I left my home in Rosarito to go to Tijuana in my truck, which broke down on the *Cuota* before I reached Tijuana. As I was waiting for help outside my truck, a weird, spaced-out man approached me. The moment I saw him I knew he was a bad man. He grabbed me, placed a knife to my throat and told me to give him my wallet. I reached back pretending to grab my wallet, but failed to bring it forward in order to play for more time. Just as I felt pressure from the knife, I heard a voice yell, "Drop it or I'll shoot." The man let go of me, running off as fast as he could go. The voice came from an off-duty policeman who happened to be driving by going the other way. He saved my life. He saw I was in trouble, ran across the four-lane road and confronted

the assailant with his police gun. He helped me obtain the necessary emergency repair for my car. Since then, I'm never without pepper spray on my belt. I recommend that everyone carry it because such incidents can happen to anyone at any time. I was lucky to have been saved by an observant policeman who had just happened to pass at the right moment. Thank you, Mister Policeman, for your courageous act of kindness!

What positive experience with the Mexican Army can be recounted?

The following incident is so preposterous it could probably never be repeated:

Rose and Maurice, Canadian pilots with their own private airplane, whimsically decided to fly from Ensenada where they live to San Quintin, a three-hour car ride south, in order to eat lunch at the Old Mill Restaurant. When they flew over the Old Mill airstrip they found it was marked with a big red X, indicating it was probably one of the small commercial airstrips closed by the Mexican government in order to control the drug trade. Disappointed, they consulted their book to find five nearby airstrips located in the San Quintin area. They naturally flew to the closest one. Surprisingly, it turned out to be professionally paved, allowing for a very smooth landing with no problem. No problem, that is, until they stopped at the end of the landing strip. Looking out the window, they nervously observed twenty gun muzzles aimed directly at them. Army soldiers dressed in full military gear surrounded their plane. One asked, in perfect Spanish with an expression of incredulous disbelief,

"Why did you land your plane in the Army airstrip?" With heart thumping, Maurice answered honestly, "We want to have lunch at the Old Mill Restaurant."

Suspicious and puzzled, the soldier led them to an official building where a man, who was obviously his superior, greeted them coldly with more questions. His temperament warmed up as Rose complimented him on a big ruby ring he wore. After a cordial conversation, Maurice finally felt comfortable enough to ask, "Could you take us to a cab so we can go to lunch at the Old Mill Restaurant?" Smiling warmly, the officer answered, "Of course, my friend. Come with me." Rose and Maurice rode with him to the gate where all the guards immediately stood at attention and saluted. With the air of someone important, he saluted back. At that moment they realized they were with an important man, the Commander of the entire base! After asking a younger soldier to take the visiting pilots to a cab, he waved farewell, turned toward the base and departed.

Rose and Maurice sighed with relief as they entered the cab that took them to the Old Mill Restaurant for lunch. The succulent food proved worthy of the effort made to obtain it. It was a delicious meal! After lunch the taxi returned the couple to the base without incident. Recognizing them as friends of the Commander, the guards allowed them to enter the gate. It was obvious a thorough searched had taken place inside the airplane while they were gone, probably for guns and drugs or maybe for a bomb, but they had nothing to hide so they didn't mind. The Army had cordially hosted the errant pilots even though they had illegally intruded upon the base. Mexican hospitality, expressed by polite manners, effectively diffused a potentially dangerous situation.

Is there an adequate fire department?

When you decide to purchase a home, check the availability of a fire department. Where is it located in proximity to your new home? The farther away, the longer it takes for them to respond to an emergency.

To illustrate my own experience with a Mexican fire department, read the following excerpt from my journal:

> The other day I heard sirens screeching behind me as I drove down the main street of Rosarito. I pulled to the side of the road as a blur of a red fire engine whizzed past in a roar of screeching sirens. "I hope the laws are the same here as in the States. The last place I want to end up is in a Mexican jail because I didn't do the right thing as a fire truck roared past me," I mused. "Whose house is burning down? It's a terrible misfortune for someone. *Pobrecito! Que Lastima!* The poor person! How sad! What a terrible misfortune for someone!" As I entered my neighborhood, I learned the identity of the unfortunate person. The fire engine was blocking the road right in front of my house! Eight Mexican firemen decked out in yellow slickers and firemen helmets were standing outside my front door. The *pobrecita* was no one other than I! My heart started to race as I thought in a panic, "Oh, no. My computer is in there full of all the words I painfully put together in sentences and paragraphs during the last year in order to create my almost completed precious book. It can't be destroyed. I can't start all over again. No, No, No!" This was a disaster for me. Not to be hindered, I told myself, "I know what I'll do. I'll just go in to save it." As I headed to the front door

to get my computer, I noticed there was no smoke pouring out of the house.

Someone stopped me saying, "You can't go in there. It's full of poisonous gas. There's no fire. At least not yet. The neighbor's propane tank is leaking . . . badly . . . foaming and sizzling while sputtering out an invisible but deadly gas right into your open windows. You'll die if you breathe that gas."

I looked at my front door. Actually it was my only door. I looked at the hissing tank. Only three feet of cement porch separated my door from the gurgling monster. I thought of the blaze that would destroy everything I owned if someone lit a match . . . or turned on the electricity causing a spark to fly.

"The firemen cut off the electricity to the house and now they're waiting for the gas company to bring a new tank," another person informed me. I watched the firemen place water-soaked rags around the sizzling, corroded hole, thus plugging up the leak. Finally they removed the entire tank, carrying it cautiously like pall bearers to the waiting gas truck that had seemed to take forever to arrive. A new tank eventually replaced the old. That was the end of poisonous gas entering into my place.

Before the firemen left, I lined them up for snapshots. They casually posed in their firemen gear, standing next to each other with broad smiles on their faces. Their expressions showed joy in completing a hazardous job successfully. They then climbed into their respective positions on the fire truck, waving a cheery good-bye as the truck rolled down the road out of sight. As I aired out my place, my nerves experienced relief while my heart filled with gratitude for those men who responded so valiantly to my neighbor's call of distress. They diffused a *muy peligroso* or very dangerous situation that could have cost me an entire year's work or, if left unattended, my own life. I shuddered at the possibility of the event happening in the middle of the night as I unknowingly slept. I decided that timing was everything. I was being watched over by God. Thank you, God. Thank you, Rosarito fire department.

Is Mexican punishment of crime different than in the United States?

Yes. It is based on the Napoleonic Code meaning that innocence must be proven, not guilt. You are considered guilty until proven innocent. Case law is ignored and printed law is considered. The jails are unpleasant and sentencing of habitual criminals who have committed three or more crimes is harsh. A judge routinely will hand out twenty-year sentences. There is no parole opportunity. Those who have money can often offer a bribe to get out of jail, but the government is trying to change this *mordida* or bribery practice. Those who participate in bribery are subject to severe punishment.

Does Baja California have a high crime rate?

The Northern Baja California area has a very low crime rate. The crime rate in all of Baja California is about one-seventh the crime rate in San Diego. The population is safer in this area than in most cities in the United States! At least the incidents of murder, rape and violent crimes are rare. When they do occur, they're most likely connected to drug trade.

Most of the towns are dependent upon the tourist trade for a major portion of their economy. If crime were rampant, it would be quickly curtailed.

The police do an excellent job in keeping the holiday crowds under control. They search cars as they enter the town and quickly jail anyone causing trouble. Fights occasionally occur among young American holiday visitors who party in bars during weekends. One night spent in the crammed conditions of a Mexican jail usually teaches a tough lesson. The residents support the quick reaction of the police. It is not the Mexican locals who cause the problems, nor is it the American residents living in Baja California.

Are there gangs in Baja California?

No. However, if members of a gang visit Rosarito from the United States, they will be swiftly disarmed and put under control by the Mexican police. Consequently, they are not likely to return with malice again.

Will taxi cab drivers attack clients?

This crime has NOT occurred in Northern Baja California, although such incidents have been reported in Mexico City.

Are there reasons to fear Mexicans?

No. In fact, if you told a Mexican you feared him, he would laugh and ask an incredulous, "Why?" Generally Mexicans are not malicious, materialistic or thoughtless. Cruelty or even selfishness isn't a part of their lives. They're a peaceful, gentle people who love their families and their God. In fact, with pure charity in their hearts, not expecting anything in return, they would stop to help a person in need. If they have a bag of food, they'd share it with those they love. I've been the recipient of many unexpected gifts. I remember being given a sack full of onions by one generous lady who had just acquired a huge sack of them. Others will drop over with freshly cooked tamales or tomatoes. Sharing and helping others is a way of life for them. A few bad people shouldn't be generalized to be all.

Linda Dobson tells the following story:

> I had a flat tire one time when I was on a freeway in San Diego. I couldn't believe a half hour went by before anyone stopped to help me. I found myself thinking, "Oh, I wish this had happened in Mexico where I live. Five minutes wouldn't have gone by before I received help if I were there."

What activities are against the law?

The following illegal activities are listed in the Secretary of Tourism's pamphlet to tourists:

- drinking in public
- disturbing the peace or being a public nuisance

- fighting
- urinating in public
- nudity or immoral conduct

It's a federal crime to:

- possess firearms
- possess, consume or import drugs

Do cars get stolen off the streets?

This crime is probably Northern Baja California's greatest problem. In one case a car disappeared while parked in a guarded neighborhood. Upon investigation, the culprits were found to be American residents from Los Angeles, not local Mexican residents.

Note:
- This car was not protected with The Club or a security alarm system nor was it parked in a garage.

- Security has been tightened and police patrols increased since this incident. No other car thefts have been reported in that particular neighborhood.

- The punishment for car theft is severe in Mexico.

Is it dangerous to camp on the beaches?

Common sense should always be used. Camping alone is not recommended. Murders and rapes are not crimes that occur very often in Baja California, Mexico. However, to be cautious, look for campgrounds along the free road between Rosarito and Ensenada. They are used by the local residents and have a nightly fee of approximately $5.

The Mexican locals camp on the sandy beaches in downtown Rosarito on holidays. They have bonfires on the beach, sharing the fun with young and old family members.

How safe is it to travel south of Ensenada?

Baja California and Baja California Sur are Mexican states located on the Baja peninsula. A ferry provides access to the mainland of Mexico. Traveling south of Ensenada on the Baja peninsula is not the same as traveling south on the mainland. Thousands of tourists travel south down the Baja peninsula without any negative incidents. Once in a while crimes will occur, just as in the States. Being at the wrong place at the wrong time is a matter of coincidence. Not making foolish decisions is the key to personal safety.

Steps are being taken to rid the Baja California area of crime.

The following letter to the editor was published in the July/August 1998 *Discover Baja* publication:

Dear *Discover Baja*,
San Quintin criminal problems became noticeable several years ago. Increased crime was due to population influx, drugs and police/judicial system corruption.

At the end of 1997, two major events triggered reform in San Quintin: 1) The deaths of two Nevada men near

El Rosario focused US media attention on the San Quintin area crime problem. 2) The local population got fed up with crime when a school was robbed of children's lunches and school equipment. The teachers, parents, and children made a protest march that was joined by local citizens.

The locals formed a group, Baja Californios, to voice their demands. In January 1998, a protest meeting was staged outside the government offices, demanding crime reform. The government responded. Crime reform came, with the replacement, reorganization and strengthening of the police and judicial system in San Quintin, Baja California.

The crime reforms have made an amazing and immediate difference with respect to the criminal activities in this area. We are happy to report that crime in our area is almost nil. Hopefully, these reforms will be long lasting. Time will tell.

—Juanita Peterman Cortez
San Quintin, BCS

The above letter is good news to travelers in Baja California. Crime is not to be tolerated. San Quintin is located in Baja California, 112 miles south of Ensenada on the Pacific Ocean.

Do homes get robbed?

Just as in the States homes will every now and then be robbed when not protected, if a thief is around. Usually protection comes in the form of just occupying a home, but many part-timers leave homes unattended since they're used as vacation retreats. In many areas home-owner's associations will pay for a common guard who screens those who come and go, thus eliminating random break-ins. Security alarm systems, high fences and locks are recommended precautions as added protection, although many homes without such protection are perfectly safe. One never knows.

Another form of robbery occurs from time to time when domestic help slowly pockets one little item at a time while working in a home. The following story illustrates how one home owner put a stop to such thievery:

> When I remodeled my home, I hired a local contractor to do the work. I paid much of the total bill in the beginning which I'd never recommend because I was consequently locked into a continued relationship with him, even when I realized that he and/or his workers were freely stealing items from my home time after time. While one person kept me busy talking to him, another would slip into the house to take what he wanted. As one item after another disappeared I became so livid I decided it was time to put a stop to it. I bought a package of ExLax and proceeded to make a special kind of chocolate candy that I placed in an empty popular chocolate box. They looked innocently delicious up in the cupboard behind canned goods, where I was certain they'd be found since taking the less obvious was their M.O. Sure enough, when I checked the cupboard after a workday, the box was obviously pillaged. During the next few days the workers did not come to work. When I saw them again, one of them was sitting on a donut cushion in his truck. He

told me they were very sick and that he would turn me into the authorities. I warned them that if they did so, I wouldn't hesitate to press thievery charges against all of them. They then left me alone. Later my cleaning lady said the chocolates made her sick. She was stealing from me too! I fired them all including the cleaning lady. From that time on I was known in town as the home owner who had "special" chocolates in his cupboard. The honest people who supplied hardware and lumber to the workmen had observed the dishonesty for years and applauded my revenge. Everyone felt they deserved what I did to them and laughed heartily about it for many months. I hope they learned the lesson that crime doesn't pay! In my mind a thief is an immoral person who deserves what he gets.

Another person states:

I rent my condo out on the weekends to vacationers who like to enjoy the beauty of the ocean. When I'd check up after they left, I couldn't figure out why the laundry detergent continually needed to be replaced. I just figured the maid used too much for each load, not understanding the correct measurement to use each time a load of sheets and towels were cleaned. I started locking up the full container, only leaving out the amount needed each time she came. That seems to have solved the problem.

How safe is it in Northern Baja California Mexico?

The following letter was written by a Baja 500 racer to the

Baja Sun newspaper when some of the racers wanted to avoid Baja California because of the "crime."

. . . Most of the veterans who have traveled Baja for many years think that it is still the place to go and visit. The warm and friendly people more than offset any criminal element. We feel there is less to fear in Baja than almost any U.S. city. The general feeling is that most people get involved with problems in Baja because they don't think and act in a safe manner. They must use common sense. Common sense tips, like those you provide for travelers, should be used by all who visit your great peninsula and they too will return home with that warm feeling of having visited a friendly neighbor.

—Tom Wimberly
Lubbock, Texas, USA

The editor answered:

In view of the economic situation and today's reality there is a unilateral increase in crime worldwide; Baja is no exception. However, the crime rate in Baja cities and rural areas is still 10 to 20 times less than any comparable city or area in the USA. This is not to make the USA bad nor to discourage people from going to the USA, but it is a fact that our friends and neighbors in that great country to the north of Mexico must by nature compare the two countries. Mexico and Baja are simply safer! Thank you for your letter.

—Editor

Do Mexicans feel safe in the United States?

It's interesting to note that when some Mexican citizens travel to the United States, they fear they are exposing themselves to crimes because they've heard news reports on the television or radio of one brutal murder, rape or robbery after another. They know those violent crimes are not as senseless or as prevalent where they live in Mexico.

When Mexicans are killed by the American border patrols, it erodes feeling of trust toward American officials.

Note: Mexico covers a large geographic area. Baja California residents don't experience much political violence but occasionally drug-related violence erupts.

What do I do to become a legal immigrant in Mexico?

The visa requirements listed below are timely general recommendations that may fluctuate and change before this book goes to print. You should consult with authorities at either a Mexican immigration office or Mexican consulate closest to the town in which you live. You also could consult with a Mexican immigration lawyer who can do the paperwork for you. Be aware that different offices require different copies of information depending upon the whim and mood of the official who services you. For instance, the Rosarito immigration office asks for you to copy every page in your passport including all the blanks or asks you to get paperwork apostilled (see page 200 for definition), while consulates don't ask for more than two copies of the photo page of a passport.

The following notice was posted in our Rosarito post office:

> **Important Notice** to all foreign citizens living permanently in Playas de Rosarito, Baja California. The local delegation of the National Institute of Immigration in Playas De Rosarito invites all foreign citizens residing permanently in this city to come to our offices which are located next to the post office in downtown Rosarito to legalize your migratory status in this country. Office hours: Monday-Friday 10:30-13:00. Instituto Nacional De Migracion Local Del. I.N.M. Playas De Rosarito, B.C. Mexico.

Obviously, many foreigners are living in Northern Baja California, Mexico, illegally. It is as serious to be illegal in Mexico as it is to be an illegal immigrant in the United States. There are many legal options available to a foreigner. None require giving up citizenship in the United States. When a renewal of a visa is required, it must be completed in the town in which a foreigner resides.

What are the phone numbers of the Mexican consulates in some of the primary locations in the United States and Canada?

The following selected numbers may not include the phone number of your specific town. Look in your phone book under "**Consulate-Mexicana**" or "**Consul General de Mexico.**" If you can't find it, phone the **Mexican Government Tourism** office in Washington, D.C., at (202) 728-1750 or any one of the consulates listed below. They will probably fax or mail a list of the phone numbers of all Mexican consulates in the US:

Arizona—Phoenix (602) 242-7398
California—Los Angeles (213) 351-6800;
        San Diego (619) 231-8414.
Florida—Miami (305) 716-4979
Illinois—Chicago (312) 855-1380
Michigan—Detroit (313) 567-7713
New York—New York City (212) 689-0456
Oregon—Portland (503) 274-1442
Texas—Dallas (214) 630-7341
Washington—Seattle (206) 448-352
Canada—Toronto (416) 368-2875

What could happen to me if I don't get a proper visa?

The following is an excerpt from the *Baja Sun* newspaper written by T.M. Bircumshaw:

> If you have purchased a home or residence of any kind or if you signed a long-term rental or lease agreement or have your own furniture in your domicile in Mexico (Baja) and are no longer a "Tourist," then according to Mexican Constitutional law you must have an FM-3 *Rentista*. This permit is most easily obtained at the Mexican Consular office closest to your U.S. residence. If you have given that up then go to the Mexican Consular office on India Street in San Diego to apply. There are certain income requirements and forms to fill out. With the proper forms you can get the permit in a couple of days. Check with the Mexican Consulate office in San Diego for the current costs and necessary forms.

I cannot make this strong enough to tell you that without this permit you are no more legal in Mexico and have no more rights than those unfortunate Mexicans who have crossed the US-Mexican border illegally and are now residing and attempting to work in the USA. If you are discovered living here in Mexico without proper authority you are subject to immediate deportation and expulsion from Mexico without any recourse whatsoever. . . . You may very well leave without any of your personal belongings including your car, clothes, furniture, bank account (if you have one), jewelry, whatever. . . . And you may be forbidden under penalty of incarceration to ever return to Mexico! Why would you want to take such a chance? Why place yourself at such risk?

What is a tourist visa or *No Inmigrante Turista*?

Valid for up to six months, a tourist visa is required by all foreigners who travel through Mexico with the exception of those who have other visas or those who travel in the Tecate-Tijuana-Rosarito-Ensenada area for a maximum of 72 hours. This northern area is considered a "free zone" for visitors for that length of time but no longer. A tourist visa is good for a maximum of six months but a new one can be obtained by leaving Mexico at the end of six months and returning with a new one. Each visa must be stamped with an official stamp at an authorized immigration office. A certified birth certificate, voter registration card or passport must be shown when an application is made. Presently, there is a $15 fee for persons traveling south of Ensenada. Those who do not travel beyond Ensenada do not have to pay the fee. When you apply for this visa, be prepared for the following questions: How long do you intend to stay? Where are you going? How are you traveling? A form will need to be filled out which you will be given as a tourist visa. Be certain to carry it with you at all times. You are not being given the right to work in Mexico, only to travel. The moment you rent, buy a home or work in Mexico, you need a different visa.

What is an FM-3?

An FM-3 is also called a *No Inmigrante Visitante Rentista*. It is a one-year residency permit allowing a person to reside in Mexico as a non-immigrant who is living on funds generated outside Mexico. It's the visa many retirees obtain. It must be renewed in Mexico each year. To obtain it the following are required:

◆ Valid passport

◆ Two pictures, front view without glasses, passport size

◆ Bank statement showing monthly earnings of at least $1000

◆ Fees: $70 and $29 (This fee is only for certain nationalities)

Note: You may be asked for copies of the passport pictures, two right profile pictures in addition to the shot of the front, a copy of a recent bank statement verifying an account in a Mexican bank and showing a deposit of $1200 for a single person or $1500 for a couple, in addition to a certified document showing ownership or a lease/rental agreement.

What is an FM-3 for Technicians and Business People?

This visa is issued to those who wish to work in Mexico. The following are required:

♦ Valid passport

♦ Two pictures, front view without glasses, passport size

♦ For business people—letter describing the type of business that a person will be doing in Mexico.

♦ For technicians—letter from company stating the type of work that the person will be doing in Mexico and his/her salary that will be paid by that same company

♦ Fees: for business people: $70; for technicians: $114; plus $29 for some nationalities that aren't exempt

It could take 30 days to obtain this type of visa. It's suggested that if a family is going to live in Mexico, a tourist visa could be used until the visa is issued. If children will be attending school in Mexico, you need to certify (apostille) their birth certificates and all the official documents that are necessary to leave the country in order to be valid in Mexico.

The above information has been taken from the Consulate of Mexico in Portland, Oregon.

Note: Requirements and fees may change at any time.

What is the process to get documents apostilled?

An apostilled document is an authenticized or legalized public document issued in the country of origin. The Secretary of the State certifies a document from the state from which it originated. For instance, take a certified copy of a US birth certificate that you obtained from the county recorder's office to the Secretary of State so that it can be apostilled or verified as being legal. The document must then be notarized by an official notary and then translated from English into Spanish by an official Mexican translator who has been certified by the State Superior Court. When this process is complete, you have an acceptable, legal document to present to the Mexican immigration authorities. In San Diego the Secretary of State's office is located at 1350 Front Street, Suite 2060, San Diego, Calif. Phone number: (619) 525-4113. In Oregon the address is 255 Capital St. N.E., Suite 151, Salem, Oregon 97310-1327. Phone number: (503) 986-2228. In Washington the address is PO Box 40220, Olympia, Wash. 98504-0220. Phone number: (360) 753-7124.

What is an FM-2?

An FM-2 is also called an *Inmigrante Rentista*. It is issued to those who apply after five years of renewing an FM-3. It is issued by immigration in Mexico City but can only be processed through the local Mexican immigration office. This visa changes the status of a person to a permanent resident alien. No more annual renewals are necessary but it still does not permit you to work.

Note: If your banking documents for earnings are generated from the United States, you have to first take them in addition to a form called a Certified Copy by Document

Custodian which verifies you're representing a truth, to an accredited notary public in the States. Second, the notarized forms need to go to the county recorder's office to be stamped to verify that the notary public is legitimate and in good standing. Third, all of these forms and documents need to be apostilled at the Secretary of State's office. Fourth, they have to be translated into Spanish in Mexico by a certified translator. Fifth, they will be ready to submit to the migration office in Mexico. All this running around for verification as described above could be avoided by setting up a bank account in Mexico that will show monthly deposits of income totaling $670 per month if you have a *Fideicomiso* or bank trust as a single person or $1500 as a couple. That required amount is doubled if you don't have a bank trust in place. Verification from a Mexican bank is a simple procedure. Be aware that it's possible to have an account in dollars that won't receive Mexican high interest rates but also won't be effected by peso devaluation.

What is an *Inmigrado* Visa?

An *inmigrado* is an immigrant. This document is a visa issued for permanent resident status that offers all the rights of a Mexican citizen except voting rights. You can own a business or work. It is only issued in Mexico City after you have had an FM-2 renewed for five years.

What is an FM-N?

This visa is also called the NAFTA visa and can be issued at the border port of entry. It allows you to work in Mexico for 30 days on behalf of a United States or Canadian

202 · BAJA FOR YOU

employer as long as pay is not generated inside Mexico. This is an easy visa to obtain.

How can I obtain Mexican citizenship?

The Mexican government doesn't make getting Mexican citizenship an easy process. It is protective of its own citizenship. It takes five years of residency in Mexico from the time you receive an FM-3 to receive an FM-2 and five years after that to get the status of *inmigrado* which allows a foreigner to work, have some ownership rights, but not to vote.

In March 1998, a new Mexican law was passed stating that a foreign person who has at least one parent who was born in Mexico can obtain citizenship. The certified birth certificate of that parent is a necessary requirement, in addition to certified and apostilled marriage and birth certificates from the country from which the person applying originates. This is not an easy process either, but it requires no residency time frame and it opens the door for descendants with Mexican blood to return to Mexico.

Note: This is a new law that is not known to all Mexican immigration officials. Don't give up if one official makes it difficult. The Mexican consulate in any United States city can guide you through the process. They help you fill out forms and then mail the application off to Mexico City. Likewise, an immigration office in Mexico can offer aid. Currently the application fee is $12.

Is it possible to have dual citizenship?

Yes. It's possible to have dual citizenship. A Mexican lawyer verified that both the United States and Mexico will honor taxes paid to one country or the other so that double taxation doesn't occur. If you make money in Mexico you may choose to pay Mexican taxes on that money or US taxes, but you have to show proof of Mexican payment to the US IRS. You would have two passports. You do give up the right to American Consulate help. You can't be officially shielded by that umbrella, although if you have both passports how would one or the other know if you only show one or the other? It's still possible continue going through the border as often as you wish with your US passport.

Whom do you recommend as an immigration lawyer?

There are many complications in the process of immigration. To avoid common pitfalls and to speed up the process, consult with a recommended Mexican lawyer. The hassle it saves is well worth the cost. Jorge Galvez is an excellent immigration lawyer in Tijuana.Call (011-52)-66-864-2992 or (619) 491-5122, US pager.

C H A P T E R E L E V E N

COMMUNICATION

This area of Mexico is a very dynamic region. Telecommunications comes before economic growth. Without economic growth telecommunications cannot grow. This region deserves the service we are trying to provide.

—Carmelo Estrada Sobrino
Telnor's Director of Finance and Administration

What can I expect for telephone service in Baja California?

Don't expect the telephone services to be the same as in the States. If you want a phone in your residence, it costs approximately $135 if you apply directly at the Telnor Company. If you're purchasing a line off a main line to a specific development from the developer, the charges could be up to $500 or more for your line. If it's new service, the cost of the poles and equipment plus the number of residents requesting service determines the fee.

Do not expect a hook-up to occur within days of sign up. It will most likely take between three and four weeks. However, I know of people who have had to wait for months. It just depends on where you are located and how much current demand takes precedence.

When purchasing a home in Baja California, it is recommended that you check out the availability of the phone lines to the residence. If there's an existing line, include leaving it and the current number as a condition of your purchase agreement. Don't just assume it will be left behind. It will save you a lot of time, money and hassle.

How do I avoid expensive long distance rates?

Most public phones in Mexico are user-friendly if you buy a Ladatel Card from a *Farmacia* or other business in town for approximately $20 or $30 per card. A phone card with time on it, like a credit card, makes local calls hassle free. Be aware, however, that long distance can charge up to $1.65 per minute. That charge is outrageous but it isn't the rip-off OAN service is. Beware of any public phone that is labeled "Call collect or use a credit card." Ask about the charges before using it, because they charge up to $27 for the first three minutes and approximately $5 for each additional minute. The Ladatel Card sounds reasonable in comparison.

Hint: Calling collect may be cheaper yet. Check it out.

If you're lucky enough to have a phone in your residence, you may want to use a long distance carrier that will cut costs, especially if you make numerous international calls. Call Victor at (011-52-66) 313812. Tell him Roberta sent you. A call-back long distance computer located in the States will cut charges dramatically. You pay a sign-up fee of $50 and a deposit of $100. Costs of long distance phone calls are then subtracted from that deposit at $0.28 per minute.

It's wise to shop around.

It's possible to have a San Diego phone number that rings in Mexico. Call Brian Hatch at BT&T Bilingual Telephone & Telecommunications at 661-3-07-87.

Most residents of Mexico are looking forward to using a satellite phone connection, which may be available by the time this book is in print. Check it out.

Will my calling card work in Mexico?

If you have the following calling cards you can access:

♦ MCI: 01-800-021-1000

♦ AT&T: 01-800-112-2020

♦ SPRINT: 01-80-877-8000

Be certain the public phone you use says Ladatel.

How do I direct dial into Mexico from the United States?

Dial these numbers in sequence:

♦ 011—access to international lines

♦ 52—country of Mexico

♦ 2-3 digit number—city

♦ 5-6 digit number—local number

What are city code numbers?

♦ **Baja Norte:**

66-Tijuana	661-Rosarito	665-Tecate
61-Ensenada	65-Mexicali	657-San Felipe
615-Bajamar, Santo Tomas, Punta Banda		
616-San Quintin		

♦ **Baja Sur:**

112-La Paz, East Cape	113-Loreto	114-Los Cabos
114-Todos Santos	115-Guerrero Negro, Santa Rosalia, Mulege	

I place a list of the above near my phone for calling convenience. Local long distance charges are expensive. Many will communicate via E-mail to avoid these charges.

What are emergency numbers?

	Rosarito & Tijuana	Ensenada
◆ **Police**	060	066
◆ **Fire**	068	060
◆ **Red Cross**	066 ambulance	066
◆ **Cellular phone**	911	911

How do I access local phone numbers?

To access Rosarito locally from Rosarito, make a seven digit number out of the existing five digit by number by adding 61 in front of it: 61 + 5 digit number.

What numbers do I dial to call the US or Canada?

◆ Dial 001 + area code + local number

How do I access long distance calls within Baja?

◆ Dial 01 + city code + local number

How do I access long distance person-to-person?

◆ Dial 02 + city code + local number for Mexico

◆ Dial 09 + city code + local number for the United States or Canada

How do I access long distance through an operator?

◆ Dial 020 for Mexico

◆ Dial 090 for international

How do I access a Mexican 800 number from within Mexico?

◆ 01 + 800 + number

What are additional special service phone numbers?

◆ exact time—030

◆ information—040

◆ phone service (line maintenance)—050

◆ Telnor—01-800-025-25-25

What are Rosarito government phone numbers?

◆ Municipal Council— (01-66) 20333 or 21351

◆ Public Security Office— 21110

◆ Family Protection Municipal Office—30080

Note: Remember to place the 61 in front of each 5 digit number for local calls.

What is the phone number of the public taxi cabs?

♦ Green-Gold Cabs—2-18-63

What quirks concerning telephone charges from Telnor should I know?

♦ Check your bill—you are charged for busy and no answer calls. It won't do any good to challenge this policy. Just be aware of it.

♦ You are charged for any 1-800 numbers you call—check your bill to see how much.

♦ It's cheaper to make calls on Sundays all day or at night between 10 PM and 8 AM—by 63% for long distance within Mexico. Between 5 PM and 10 PM—you save 20% for long distance within Mexico on weekdays.

♦ Long distance to US is 33 % less on weekends or evenings after 7 PM.

♦ Telnor offers a special long distance rate for calling California area codes in the San Diego area. Area codes 619 and 760 will cost $0.21 per minute if you request a Unilada discount.

♦ You must request it by calling the service department at 01-8-000-252525 or 332308. Check your first bill to see if it is set up correctly.

♦ A 10% tax is added on all bills.

♦ You are allowed 200 minutes of local calls per month. Any minutes above that time you are charged $0.04 per minute.

Are American phone companies established in Mexico?

A powerful company called Telnor operated for at least 15 years without competition. In 1997, however, Telnor's franchise area opened to competition. It maintains dominance in Northern Baja California, but AT&T is available for long distance service. Check out current competitive pricing. Don't assume AT&T will offer better rates.

"Telmex, its subsidiaries and several US telephone companies are currently laying a fiber optic line from Guaymas, across the Sea of Cortez, then southward to Los Cabos." Quote from Bliss Richards, webmaster for bajaquest.com

The above line will not help Baja California Norte, but it indicates the forward motion of the communication systems in Mexico.

Is it possible to make phone calls from a home computer?

If you own a computer with a sound card, speakers and a microphone, you can download for free a program that allows calls to the United States and Canada. 800 or 888 numbers are free except for Internet charges. The person who receives the call uses a normal phone to answer. You can download the Net2 phone program at: http://www.net2phone.com. Normally from Mexico 800 or 888 numbers cost 10 to 15 cents per minute depending upon the time of day.

What can I keep by the phone to remind me of how to dial in Mexico?

A copy of the following can be made to tape onto the phone until you learn the numbers:

From US to Mexico:
011+52+(# of city)+(local number)
66—Tijuana
661—Rosarito
61—Ensenada

To US from Mexico: 01+area code+local number

Long distance calls within Mexico:
01+city code+(61 for Rosarito)+ local number

US 800/888 number from Mexico:
001-880 (drop 1-800)
001-881 (drop 1-888)

Mexican 800 number from Mexico:
01-800+ number

What are some useful Ensenada phone numbers?

Place (011-52-61) before the following numbers when calling from the US.
Ensenada Convention and Visitor's Bureau—78-2411
City Police—060 or 76-2421
Fire Department—068
Police—060

214 · BAJA FOR YOU

Red Cross—066
Green Angels—76-4675
Transmedic Ambulance—78-1400
    (or toll free within Mexico—01-800-026-3342)
State Police—72-3072
Federal Police—76-1311
Roads and Bridges—74-6081
Immigration—74-0164
Customs—74-0897
US Consulate (in Tijuana)—(66) 81-7400
Ensenada Tourism Trust—1-800-310-9687

What can I expect from the postal service in Baja California?

Americans in Tijuana and Rosarito have the luxury of avoiding the Mexican postal service because the US border is so close. The Mexican postal system is not consistent, causing mail delivery to be delayed for days and sometimes weeks. This can cause havoc with bills to pay and businesses to run. How have American residents resolved this problem? Some enterprising people have started private mail services. **The Mail Room**, next to René's Restaurant, located at the south end of town, costs $12 per month for a private PO box. Dick Armand, the owner, goes across the border three times a week on Monday, Wednesday and Friday to pick up and deliver mail from a San Ysidro, California, address. His phone number is: (661) 2-1974. Tell him Roberta sent you.

Another mail service is **Mail Express and Xtras**, located on a side street across the street from the address. Rosarito Beach Hotel. Call 011-52-661-2-2423. They offer:

- daily mail service

- telephone message service

- fax sending or receiving

- shipping outlet

- laminating

- key duplication

- copy service

- greeting cards

Feel free to ask local residents for recommendations.

Where is the Rosarito Mexican post office located?

The post office is on Calle Acacias off the main street in Rosarito. Be sure to purchase Mexican stamps here and find out what it costs to mail to the US if you choose to use the Mexican postal service. The postal zip codes are:

Tijuana—22000-22699
Ensenada—22800-22899
Rosarito—22710

Is Internet connection possible in Northern Baja California?

Yes. The Internet has become a vital necessity for communication around the world. Many individuals and businesses

have become dependent upon it as a daily method of interacting with the world either through E-mail or World Wide
informational Web. Clients can be found and nurtured
through this medium, which has effectively transformed
worldwide commerce.

Providers in Northern Baja California are:

♦ **Telnor.net**—Call 01-800-025-2525 for information.
   E-mail: info@ telnor.com

♦ **Icanet**—Call (619) 428-0055 from the USA or
   84-8305 from Tijuana

♦ **Satellite**—Call Comp USA Direct for information
   about satellite service. 1-800-669-4727
   E-mail: mrc@compusadirect.com

♦ **Compuserve**—The Mexican access phone number for
   those who are set up as a Compuserve users is:
   01-8007200-00 from Mexico and 1-800-848-8199
   for customer support in the United States.

♦ **Micro Soluciones de Ensenada**

Ask local residents what connections they use. It's a fast-
moving industry that evolves and improves continually.
For a list of Internet providers in all of Mexico see:
http://www.mty.itesm.mx/MexWeb

Beware: I tried a provider that wanted to keep my laptop
overnight in order to install their program. They returned
the computer damaged but would not be responsible for it.
I now have a policy of not letting my laptop out of my
sight. Anyone who touches it has to come highly recommended. (Check on page 218 for a technician who can be
trusted in Tijuana.)

Be aware that the phone company charges for local time used on their lines. Internet use is not as inexpensive as in the United States.

Can I use an Internet connection for a cellular phone?

Alpha Com promotes an Internet service for wireless modem access to the Internet with cellular technology. Current costs are $399 for the modem, $134 flat fee per month, not per minute. Access currently available in Tijuana only. Call Sam Warren, (66) 80-10-52.

Are there any public establishments that offer Internet connections?

♦ **Ensenada**—**Internet Café** offers Internet access.
Ave Juarez 1449-8. Open Monday-Saturday 9 AM–9 PM
Sunday 1 PM-9 PM
Telephone for more information: 61-76-13-31.

♦ **Tijuana**—Space Café is located in Las Playas in Tijuana.

♦ **Rosarito**—now has public computer rental service at a business called **Mi PC** located on Calle Cleofas Ruiz #21 one block off Benito Juarez across from the Rosarito Beach Hotel. Computer use is charged by the minute or hour. Phone 612-36-39 for more information or E-mail: mipc@telnor.net

Try this website for a list of cybercafes and bulletin boards to keep in touch while traveling through Mexico: http://www.weblane.com/experiencia/bb/

Whom do I call when I need computer service?

In **Ensenada** call: **Compuclub**—offers parts and is a provider—01-617-761-331

In **Rosarito** call: **Jackie Alameda**—offers personal service, as needed—01-661-21550

In **Tijuana** call: **PC-Tech-Daniel Orozco**—excellent service in repair, maintenance, set-up etc. Call 01-66-482-482

Where can I purchase computer programs or equipment?

PC Tech in Tijuana can set up and train you to use the computer. Call Daniel at 01-66-482-482.

A **Costco Price Club** is now in Tijuana. Everything from scanners to paper to software is available. It's located on the road to Tecate. Just follow the Tecate directions off Ave. de Los Heroes. Drive alongside the river until you see the building on the right.

Note: Products from the United States are more expensive in Mexico because of the tariff placed upon imported items.

Is it possible to continue my computer education?

One of the benefits of living close to the border is being able to take advantage of the San Diego area seminars. Join the **Learning Annex** in order to receive monthly listings of upcoming classes taught by talented and famous people such as:

How to Create Your Own Website, How to Become a Webmaster, Learn About JavaScript, VRML, XML & more or **Introduction to FrontPage 98.**

A multitude of topics outside of the subject of the computer is also offered. These words are written in the brochure: "Do you have a group of four or more? Take advantage of course savings. Call for special rates." Call (619) 544-9700 or fax (619) 544-9734.

What are the addresses of websites that offer further information about Baja California?

There are a variety of sites, too numerous to list here. These are my favorites:

http://www. geocities.com/Baja/
> *Los Baños de Baja*—laugh with us as we travel through a pictorial journey of bathrooms found along the way down the Baja Peninsula

http://www.bajaquest.com
> The music, graphics, information and bulletin boards on this site are user-friendly. Baja interests from fishing to insurance are featured.

http://www.bajasun.com
> This is a webpage for the *Baja Sun* newspaper. Current information is presented about Baja California and Baja California del Sur.

http://www.bajasun.com/mapman.htm
> Maps are available to view and to order.

http://www.discoverbaja.com
> This site offers membership into a club with an advertising motto of: "You can count on our 30 years of Baja

experience." They offer discounts on travelers' needs.

http://www.baja4u.com

This site is for all those who have real estate needs in Northern Baja California, Mexico. It is my site. You can order copies of this book. Inquire about discounts for quantity orders and ask about my seminar schedule. You may schedule me as a speaker or attend a local lecture. E-mail questions or feedback to: baja4u@hotmail.com

http://www.rosaritobch.com

This site contains information about Rosarito Beach with listings of hotels, restaurants, shops and night spots. Phone numbers and addresses are included.

http://www.mexico-trade.com

Technical, legal information concerning "Mexico Business Opportunities and Legal Framework" is offered in a reader-friendly format. Anyone wanting to do business with or in Mexico will appreciate this site.

http://www.mexconnect.com

This site has excellent articles about Mexico as well as general and business bulletin boards offering valuable information.

http://www.greenbuilder.com/mader/mexico

Environmental articles offered and unusual websites listed. Ecotourism defined.

C H A P T E R   T W E L V E

HEALTH CONCERNS

If I keep a green bough in my heart . . .
The singing birds will come
—Anonymous

Can I buy medical prescriptions in Mexico?

Farmacias or pharmacies can be found easily in Baja California. It is possible to purchase, without prescriptions, medicines that require prescriptions in the United States. Worthwhile savings are at least one-third the cost but most are substantially better.

Examples are: Retin A is $6 in Mexico, while it's $50 in the states. Inhalers for allergies are around $10 in Mexico, while $48 in the states. Hydrocortisone, antibiotics, high blood pressure pills, etc. are available without prescriptions. Self-medicating can be dangerous, but the pharmacist will guide you as he does his Mexican customers. Any drug that is illegal for him to sell without a prescription will not be available to you unless you have a prescription.

The Baja California Secretary of Tourism says, "When buying any type of medication be sure there are no restrictions for its purchase."

A word of caution: If you purchase a drug with a prescription that is illegal in Mexico to procure without one, be certain to keep the prescription with you. You may need to show it as proof if you get searched by the Mexican police at a checkpoint or at the US border on your return to the States.

Another word of caution: The following is quoted from the U.S. Customs Service:

> The United States Federal Food, Drug and Cosmetic Act, which is administered by FDA, prohibits the interstate shipment (which includes importation) of unapproved new drugs. Unapproved new drugs are any drugs, including foreign-made versions of U.S. approved drugs, that have not received FDA approval to demonstrate they meet the federal requirements for safety and effectiveness. It is the importer's obligation to demonstrate to FDA that any drugs offered for importation have been approved by FDA.

If the drug is used for personal use, the FDA may allow importation provided the following criteria apply:

♦ The patient has a serious condition for which effective treatment is not domestically available.

♦ There is no known commercialization or promotion to persons residing in the US by those involved in the distribution of the product at issue.

♦ The product is considered not to represent an unreasonable risk.

♦ The individual confirms in writing that it is for the patient's own use (generally not more than 3 months supply) and provides the name and address of the doctor licensed in the US responsible for his or her treatment, or provides evidence that the product is for the continuation of a treatment begun in a foreign country.

For further information concerning the importation of FDA unapproved prescription medicines and drugs, see this Internet site:
http://www.customs.treas.gov/travel/meds.htm

Can I trust a Mexican dentist or optometrist?

Yes, but as with anything else, don't go to someone who isn't highly recommended. Many Americans will travel to Mexico from the States on a regular basis just to get care from Mexican doctors. An added bonus is that the cost is probably less than in the United States. The following dentist has been highly recommended:

Dr. Fernando Lizarraga, Ave. Calle Delante, Ensenada, B.C.

A dentist in Rosarito has the most modern equipment, speaks English and is quite professional. Located on the main street, his name and phone number are: Dr. Oscar Avila—(011-52-661) 2-1383

In Tijuana, The Dentigroup, which is located on the Mexico side of the San Ysidro border, is capable of advanced specialized dental care. Call (619)428-0690. Ask for Dr. Juan Pablo Eng.

For biological dentistry or oral surgery, visit Dra. Corinne Vizcarra, D.D.S. in Tijuana. Call (011-52-66) 84-20-79.

What dental advice is offered by the Ensenada Dental Group?

The following article appeared in the *Baja Sun*, Dec., 1998, page 7, written by the Ensenada Dental Group, (61) 78-3777

Endodontic Treatment can save you time, money, discomfort and your very own teeth. A winning deal. Here's the Score—Inside your tooth is a tissue called pulp. This can become inflamed or infected for any number of reasons: decay, a crack or chip in the tooth or repeated dental procedures on the tooth. Left untreated, this inflamed or infected pulp can lead to pain or abscess. You may experience ongoing pain, sensitivity to hot or cold, swelling and tenderness in, or discoloration of, the tooth. Fortunately, the mature tooth does need the pulp to survive, and that's where endodontic treatment comes into play. The Game Plan—19 out of 20 endodontic treatments are fully successful the first time for a lifetime. And with modern techniques and anesthetics, you should feel no pain during the treatment. That's something to cheer about!

Dr. Miguel Angel Ortiz
Dr. Carlos Gallegos R.
Gastelum #777-7 Ensenada, B.C. Mexico
www.bajasun.com//dentalgroup.htm
E-mail: cgallegos@compunet.com.mx

What medical care is available in Baja California?

The government sets up medical clinics in each town, but local people are expected to support them through donations. The sign of the **Red Cross** easily identifies them. The Red Cross emergency phone number for Tijuana is 132; for Rosarito it's 066.

In Rosarito, the Red Cross hospital and its bilingual staff will assist in most daily needs. In the case of an emergency, ambulances are available and can coordinate with San Diego ambulances for transfer at the border. Call 2-04-14.

To join the Red Cross or Cruz Roja Mexicana organization, yearly dues are $12.50. Send it to Cruz Roja Mexicana, PO Box 433220, San Ysidro, Calif. 92143-3220. If you should fall ill or have an accident, you will be transported to a stateside hospital by ground or by air. Fundraisers such as bake sales, fashion shows, thrift shop sales as well as a Christmas Ball bring in enough money to keep the organization a valuable resource to Rosarito. (See page 277 for more information about this organization.)

What phone number should I call for general medical emergencies?

Post this number on your telephone or key it into your telephone's automatic-dial system: 01-(800) 633-42. Remember: dial 066 for ambulance service.
Also: Binational Emergency Medical Care Committee, Chula Vista, California. Call (619) 425-5080.

What hospitals are located in Rosarito?

FamilyCare de Rosarito, S.C.—This is a new clinic located on Benito Juarez in downtown Rosarito. It is associated with Sharp Hospital in San Diego and offers a well-trained medical staff and the most advanced technology. They boast that their care far exceeds that of any medical facility in the US. Everything from the food to the pharmacy is geared to the comfort and good health of the patient. A patient feels his every need is filled by trained personnel. Check with your HMO; it may be accepted by a local Mexican hospital. Talk to others who use it before joining.

Hospital Cruz Roja Mexicana—Rene Ortiz Campoy
No. 100 Zona Centro. Call 2-04-14.

I.M.S.S—Acacias No.19 y Mar del Norte Zona Centro.
Call 2-32-20.

Centro de Salud—Vista al Mar S/N Zona Centro.
Call 2-25-69

What hospitals are in Ensenada?

In Ensenada the **San Jose Hospital**, located on Chapultepec, can be reached by phoning (011-52-617)-7-47-57.

The **Baja Emergency Health Program** facility is located in Ensenada. See the following page for more information.

What hospitals are in Tijuana?

Cruz Roja is located at Alfonso Gamboa S/N 2da Etapa Zona Rio. Call 21-77-87.

Hospital General de Tijuana is located at Ave. Centenario #10851, Zona Rio. Call 84-09-22.

IMSS is located at Blvd. Agua Caliente y Fco. Sarabia S/N, Aviacion. Call 29-63-42.

ISSSTE is located at Blvd. Diaz Ordaz y Av. De Las Palmas No.1, Las Palmas. Call 81-47-40 or 44.

ISSSTECALI is located at Blvd. Diaz y Av. De Las Palmas No. 1, Las Palmas. Call 81-62-50, 81-61-35.

What air travel is available in cases of extreme emergencies?

Air Evac International is available for a flight day or night out of San Diego. Call (619) 292-5557 or 278-3822.

The **Red Cross** will assist you in any needed arrangement. Call 066.

Check out the **Baja Emergency Health Program** at 1-800-010-5076 or (011-52-617)-74-7-57. They offer US-accredited primary care in Mexico, emergency medical transport approved by the FAA and immediate transport to any San Diego hospital by **Critical Air Medicine Inc.** of San Diego, the largest exclusively air medical transport company in the US. They have a highly trained medical staff and experience in Baja California, Mexico. The acute care facility is payment-accredited by all major United States insurance companies. In fact, 65% of their patients are United States or Canadian citizens. They claim to have "state of the art" operating rooms.

Is a Kaiser Permanente Medical clinic located nearby?

Yes. A new fully serviced care center is located five minutes from the border in the state of California. The modern facility is located just off the 805 freeway at the Palm Avenue exit. Dr. Cevallos is an excellent doctor. Call (619) 528-5000 for more information. The address is 4650 Palm Avenue, San Diego, CA 92173.

Are Mexican doctors qualified physicians?

Yes. I have American friends who are very devoted patients of their Mexican doctor whom they've used successfully for years. Many Mexican doctors are accredited in the United States. They will work in conjunction with specialists whom they recommend when needed.

Is there a local doctor who is well-qualified to be my doctor?

Kathy Wasson has a doctor in Rosarito who saved her life. This remarkable doctor, *La Doctora*, who received her MD degree in Mexico City, treated Kathy for a serious condition that required a technical operation. *La Doctora* diagnosed Kathy correctly, and after extensive lab tests confirmed her diagnosis, determined an operation was essential and then sent for a specialist from Mexico City to operate. She proceeded to oversee the operation in her small Rosarito hospital that is connected to her own home. *La Doctora* closely monitored Kathy in her hospital as she recuperated after the operation. It was *La Doctora* who brought Kathy warm chicken soup, not an impersonal nurse. She would say, "Eat up. This soup will make you strong," as she coaxed Kathy to recover. Medically she was equally as solicitous to her patient. Kathy's US insurance paid for this exceptional care that would never have been equaled in the United States. "I would not have been watched over that carefully in a hospital in the United States. It was like going back in time to when a family doctor really cared for his patient by personally attending to her."

The following is another example of this doctor's ability to diagnose an ailment correctly:

Another person suffered from a ringing or buzzing in her ears that wouldn't go away. After checking her ears, her United States HMO set up an appointment with a specialist for a month in advance, telling her any earlier appointment would be impossible to schedule. That meant waiting an additional four long weeks while buzzing like an electric razor in her ears drove her to distraction. One visit to *La Doctora* and it was cured. *La Doctora* looked into her ears, said they were both inflamed and proceeded to cleanse them. She prescribed pills, saying a fungus caused an inflammation causing the annoying ringing in her ears. A simple cure at last! No other doctor diagnosed this malady correctly. In fact, she at one time was told, "Listen to soft music distract yourself from hearing the buzzing" by one doctor who thought the malady was in her mind. Not *La Doctora*. She knew what caused it and how to cure it! She has the secret to curing other diseases too. One shot in the infected area will take the pain away from arthritis.

La Doctora's name is Maria Elena Jardon, M.D. Her phone number is (011-52-661) 2-33-05. She's located on the main street of Rosarito on the south end of town, across from Rosarito Shores and next to the taxi stand.

I've heard that Mexico has many innovative alternative health programs. What is available in Baja California?

There are many government-granted research facilities available. If you have allergies, asthma, immunological intolerance, rheumatoid arthritis, lupus, Sjogren's syndrome, chronic fatigue, candidiase, herpes, mono, Epstein-Barr, cytomegalovirus infection or Aids, you may want more information about the **William Hitt Center** in Tijuana. Call (888) 671-9849. William Hitt is a renowned, award-winning physician and pioneering scientist who taught at the acclaimed McCollum-Pratt Institute at Johns Hopkins University. He is pursuing his scientific research in Mexico and has received many awards. His pamphlet states that he offers "A program that Does More Than Treat Symptoms . . . We Target the Cause of Immune Disorders." Try it. It may save your life.

The **Sanoviv Health and Healing Center** has been designed and developed by Dr. Myron Wentz to provide a nontoxic healing and caring facility for those with degenerative diseases or for those in good health who wish to maintain and improve their health. Nutrition, the mind and the immune and apoptotic defense system are assisted in the toxin-free facility located on the Pacific coast just south of Rosarito. See http://www.sanoviv.com for more information.

The California **Chelation Center** for prevention and treatment of chronic degenerative diseases such as aneurysms, gout, angina, atherosclerosis, high blood pressure, lupus, osteoarthritis, osteoporosis and rheumatoid arthritis is located in Rosarito on Benito Juarez #92. The following is quoted from their pamphlet:

> Along the years, and due to bad habits, and dietary abuses and deficiencies, we produce and accumulate several toxins that are normally expelled by our body. However, once our physiologic mechanisms are overloaded, a series of changes occur in our body, leading it to develop chronic-degenerative diseases. Chelation therapy is a safe and effective method for drawing toxins and metabolic wastes from the blood stream. Chelating agents administered intravenously have been proven to increase blood flow and remove arterial plaque (hard thickening build up from cholesterol inside the arteries). The reversal is accomplished in part

through the removal of calcium content (ions) from the artery walls.

Call (011-52) 661-2-33-05 for more information.

A unique program for vacationing patients who require hemodialysis is offered by "**Getaway Specials.**" Medical attention is given to those who need it while vacationing in Ensenada. Call (011-52-617)-6-36-14.

Aguas Termales Valparaiso Hotel and Spa offers a health program to build up immune systems. It is possible to pinpoint problem areas in the body so that a preventative cure can be implemented. The onslaught of cancer can be detected seven years in advance and the Gulf War disease can be treated. Call (011-52-66) 24-07086 for more information.

Dr. Miguel Angel Solis Miranda is a *naturista* or naturalistic doctor. Knowledge of healing herbs and plants is his specialty. Call (011-52-66) 22-07-32.

What herbs, plants and other powders do Baja California Indians and ranch people use for medicinal purposes?

Each town has a swap meet or flea market on Saturday or Sunday. In Rosarito, it is a family event to go to the swap meet. Natural medicines are sold in leaf, powder or pill form at some of the booths. Just ask. The ranchers and Indians who live away from town have survived for years on natural cures. Here is a sample list of their medicines:

- **gobernadora**—plant from which tea is made for kidney ailments

- **napales or cactus**—a special cactus that cures diabetes, arthritis, high cholesterol, cancer, and infections

- **ajos or garlic**—arthritis, intestinal parasites and can soothe insect bites.

- **snake powder**—arthritis

- **artichoke**—high cholesterol

- **sabella or aloe vera**—burns or skin rashes

- **yellow flower or lemon water**—intestinal gas

- **taraweed**—prostrate problems

- **tetohuxtle**—tea for diabetes

Andrés Meling tells of a miracle cure he witnessed while living on the Meling Ranch. A man, Jurgen Rasmusser, came to change shakes on the schoolhouse roof at the ranch. A splinter imbedded itself under the skin of his right knee. Because he tried to dig it out with a dirty pocket-knife, it festered and became infected. Within a few days it became so rotten with gangrene, he finally decided to see a doctor. The doctor recommended that his leg be amputated. He refused. Burning with fever and delirious, he called an Indian healer who washed out the sore with a mixture of household bleach and water. He used a green plant that he boiled in another tub. The healer kept pouring one solution and then another on the open holes where the gangrene had eaten through the skin. Finally, the green powder was poured directly into the holes. The next morning, the fever was gone. In another fourteen hours, he was to reapply the washing and powder. In the meantime a strong tea made of the same powder was given to him to drink. From what plant was the powder taken? It was taken from the lumboy plant that only grows in Baja California Mexico. (See page 99 for description of Andrés Meling's healing from the same plant.)

Can I get sick from drinking the water in Baja California?

This is a very common concern. Unlike mainland Mexico, most of Baja California's water is supplied by wells and has been considered safe for years. However, it is a good practice to take precautions. Many homes have filtered water, but some of the older ones do not. Filters are possible to add to an existing system, but if you purchase a home, it is wise to test a sample at a qualified water-testing facility. Call 66-82-1861 for water analysis at **Santiago Arreola Victor Tecnologico** in Tijuana. In the meantime, drinking water directly from the tap is not a good practice. I always supply bottled water for my guests to use when brushing teeth, but my husband and I brush with tap water.

Mexican federal law expects restaurants to serve purified water and ice, free of contaminants.

What is a *pila*?

A *pila* is a holding tank or water cistern. In areas where there is no public water, individual homes have a *pila* on their property, either located in the garage or backyard. Either water trucks deliver water before the *pila* empties or water comes through a public source into a *pila* operating off a pump. When buying a home, ask about the water source. The cost of filling a *pila* should be budgeted if you choose a home that depends upon truck delivery.

New subdivisions may have their private water treatment on site so the water is a neighborhood co-op concern.

Will I get sick when I return to the United States after living in Mexico?

Bodily immune systems must adapt to the local bacteria. Whenever I return to the United States, I have at least one run to the bathroom before my body readjusts to the bacteria in the States. Mexicans who travel elsewhere have the same trouble adjusting to the water away from their local area.

Where can I buy purified water?

Purified water is sold in the shopping center where Comercial, the local supermarket, is located. You provide the containers and then fill up. San Ysidro California, the border town, also has water "fill up" dispensers.

Bottled drinking water is also available by delivery trucks, just as in the US. Most homes in Mexico have bottled service delivery.

Will boiling water help to purify it?

Yes. However, it must boil for at least twenty minutes.

What can I use to purify fresh vegetables?

Either in the vegetable department in a supermarket or in a pharmacy, you can purchase *yodo* which is **iodine**. Soak the vegetables with *yodo* for at least ten minutes. Then rinse with purified water. No aftertaste will be discerned. If you use bleach, be certain to add a couple of drops to the water. Don't overdo it or you will have an aftertaste.

Always squeeze the juice of a lime on any foods you may buy in a stall or off street carts. Hygiene or refrigeration isn't always practiced and the lime juice may kill the bacteria.

What is a *fosa*?

A *fosa* is a septic tank. When purchasing a home, ask about this important feature. A septic tank shouldn't be located too close to a *pila*. It would be wise to have it tested or at least emptied before purchasing the home but that is not a common practice. Most subdivisions have a sewage recycling system for the local area. Find out where it goes and check with neighbors about how well it works.

Why are there lined wastebaskets beside the toilets in restrooms?

The wastebaskets are receptacles for used toilet paper. They are lined with a plastic bag that is often emptied. Pipes in older buildings become clogged easily with too much paper causing septic systems to malfunction. This primitive method of disposing paper is a way to prevent frustrating septic problems. Many local restaurants located in older buildings have signs asking for your cooperation with such sayings as "Please use the wastebasket for your paper." It's wise to obey. It keeps the toilet operating. I've had experiences of stepping into overflow upon entering a public restroom. Searching for an alternative place to go can be a nightmare, especially in an emergency.

A humorous comment, made by a frustrated maintenance man who had to unclog an overflowing toilet in an Ensenada restaurant, was as follows, "Those crazy Americans are just pigs! They have no proper training! They keep throwing the toilet paper into the toilet. They're pigs. Just pigs! I have to continually clean up their messes!" Interesting twist of perspective, isn't it?

If someone were to ask me what is the most difficult adjustment I have to make when I return to the United States, I'd say it's remembering to put the toilet paper into the toilet instead of into a wastebasket. I find myself subconsciously looking for the wastebasket, then realizing I'm in the United States and can now flush the paper away. I wonder what the Mexicans tourists think when they don't find the wastebasket? Please be aware that the newer subdivisions do not have problems with clogged sewer lines. They have modern systems and better pipes. However, if you move to Mexico, be certain to have a lined wastebasket in each bathroom for your Mexican friends even if you have a modern disposal system. Customs are not easily changed and there's no need to frustrate your guests.

Note: Not all public restrooms in Mexico provide toilet paper. Remember to carry a roll of toilet paper in your car. Believe me, it will come in handy some day!

Can I get sick from eating the local produce?

I enjoy the local, non-tourist restaurants and also shop in the Mexican supermarkets and farmer's markets. Although I carefully wash produce, I have yet to get sick from any. Perhaps I've developed immunity to the microbes by now.

Note: this may **not** be true of all Mexico.

Most cases of "Montezuma's Revenge" stem from lack of proper refrigeration of dairy products or from lack of proper cleanliness of food servers. It's not a common occurrence in Rosarito, but be cautious.

How can I cure Montezuma's Revenge?

Take the juice of one lime and add a half-teaspoon of baking soda; add a couple of pinches of salt when it starts to fizz. Drink it quickly and in approximately three hours the malady will be gone. Don't overdose or you'll really have troubles.

Should I have a first aid kit?

Everyone should put together an adequate first aid kit for their car and medicine cabinet in their home. Mexican pharmacies are stocked with most supplies you'll need at a more reasonable price than in the United States. Be certain to stock bandages, iodine, aspirin and vitamin C. Order the lightweight portable splint from Sam Scheinberg, M.D. Call 1-800-818-4726 or check out his Internet website: http://www.samsplint.com. Also, add herbs to your first aid kit. Some booths at the Sunday flea market will sell curing herbs more reasonably than the pharmacy. Just ask for the herbs that treat the ailment and you'll find the merchant or pharmacist will be most helpful. For instance, I told a pharmacist I have high cholesterol. He suggested that I take pills made from artichoke leaf extract.

If you don't want to mess with gathering all the necessary items for the medical kit, then order a ready-made one. The shopping mall magazine for Alaska Airlines has a compact kit for $39. Look up **Alaska sky-mall** on a site like **dogpile.com** that will search all the search engines when you press the "fetch" button.

Are insects a problem?

In Northern Baja California the weather is similar to San Diego's. Ants, termites and spiders are common in Northern Baja California, but these insects do not pose a problem.

What spas are available for mineral baths, facials or massage?

Casa Playa Spa at the Rosarito Beach Hotel offers a treatment center where *"you will experience body work that not only relaxes you but rejuvenates your inner and outer body. Personalized programs can be tailored to your needs."* Hydrotherapy baths, facials, massages, herbal wraps and a fitness gym are available to suit your needs. A 15% discount for Baja California residents is currently offered. Call the spa at (001-52-661) 2-2687 or for hotel reservations 1-800-343-8582.

Internet website address: http://www.rosaritohtl.com

Aguas Termales Valparaiso Hotel and Spa in Tijuana offers natural mineral water baths as well as body wraps, facials and massages. This facility dates back to the 1950s when Tijuana was a playground for the rich and famous, so expect it to be loaded with history and charm. It's located at Avenida de La Paz #16420, Colonia Mineral Santa Fe, Tijuana, B.C., Mexico. Call (001-52-66) 24-07086. Better ask for directions because it's tricky to locate.

Note: See page 128 for a list of local massage experts. Go ahead. Pamper yourself. In fact, the cost is so reasonable, you could do it once a week or at least once a month!

CHAPTER THIRTEEN

ANIMALS

**It's probably a surprise to many of you that there
are no leash laws here and dogs are free to cavort
with their humans on any beach, at any time of
day or night and the dogs down right love it!**
—Audre Pinque
Tourist guide, Oct. 1998

Can I bring my pets across
the border into Mexico?

Yes. Dogs and cats are allowed to cross into Mexico without any registration. It's wise to travel with a current health certificate stating that the animal is free of communicable diseases. These can be obtained from veterinarians either in the States or in Northern Baja California. A recent rabies certificate would also be smart to have. These documents may be needed at the border when the animals return, but in Mexico they're generally not necessary. For further information about customs check this Internet site: http://www/customs.treas.gov/travel/pets.htm

Can I have pets?

Don't expect all Mexican hotels to accept animals. Many establishments are leery of animals because they're considered carriers of fleas and diseases. The places that will accept pets are usually less expensive and will offer an "adventure" in local color.

Most neighborhoods don't ban residents' pets. Leash laws, noise and defecation restrictions may apply in the newer subdivisions, however.

Can I obtain a pet once I get into Mexico?

Consider adopting a Mexican dog and/or cat once you reside here. They hunger for love and affection and many are homeless. (See the section on Animal Sanctuary under charities on page 276.) An anecdote from my journal is as follows:

> Claudia, my neighbor, adopted a Mexican dog who was at first very tense and seemed to be angry at the world. I worried that he would attack me without provocation; however, after receiving love from his new owner for a few months, he relaxed into a calmer and more trusting dog. One day Claudia brought him

into my place for the first time. He ventured around the room, sniffing everything. When he started up the stairs, he stopped on the landing and tilted his head upward in the direction of a colorful painting that hung on the wall. His head moved from the top of the painting to the bottom and then back up and down one more time as if he were studying the fine details of the painting and appreciating its qualities. From that moment of observing pure intellectual appreciation, I became fond of that dog. Now when I see him I ask him to raise his paw to shake hands with me. He looks directly into my eyes and squeezes my hand with his paw. I swear there's a grin on his face too. I'll never underestimate a Mexican stray again. A little love and tender care brings out the best in all of us.

What suggestions should I follow in caring for my animals?

♦ Have tags on your animals with home address and telephone number.

♦ Keep current with vaccinations and flea elimination.

♦ Be aware that firecrackers are legal in Mexico. Guard against pets running away on holidays when firecrackers commonly are used. Be aware of the dates of Mexican holidays.

♦ Mexican-owned dogs and American-owned dogs have language differences. A Mexican dog will respond to Spanish words, while an American dog will respond to English. Also, many dogs are trained to defend homes, so train yours to avoid straying onto private property.

- Keep your dog off the road. Cars don't stop for them. Consequently, road kill is common.

- Always carry a bag and a scoop to clean up your dog's mess. No one enjoys encountering a dog's defecation.

- Dogs make excellent watchdogs for security. Consider adopting one for this purpose.

- Don't leave animals in locked cars with the windows rolled up on a hot day.

- Watch what your animals eat and drink.

- Keep your animals away from street animals. Diseases could be contagious.

How does the Mexican attitude toward dogs and cats differ from the attitude in the US?

There is a definite cultural difference in attitude. Mexicans don't consider dogs and cats part of the family as Americans do. Animals live outside to protect the home from outsiders. Cats kill rodents and dogs bark to scare strangers away. Pets in the States are valued and pampered more.

Can my animals receive adequate medical care in Mexico?

There is no need to be anxious about leaving your favorite veterinarian in the States. You'll find an excellent replacement in Mexico. As a matter of fact, you'll enjoy the grooming service that comes to your home for a reasonable price. You'll be able to afford to pamper your pets so often they'll never want to leave Mexico.

Dr. Alfonso Olvera Torres is an experienced veterinarian in Ensenada at the corner of 9th and Moctezuma. He offers grooming, medical care and pet supplies. Call (61) 74-0740.

What other animals can be pets?

I have friends who have a chicken as a pet. This chicken wanders freely all around their yard. Their house fronts to the beach. You'd think it would wander away, but it hangs around outside and survives.

Another friend has a pet iguana, while others have colorful parrots. The other day I saw a woman driving down the street with a large colorful parrot on her shoulder. She was driving slowly down a neighborhood street with a broad grin on her face.

Warning: Don't take exotic animals across the border into the US unless you want to pay an unreasonable fine and be invited to enjoy free room and board, compliments of the federal prison bureau.

Do Mexican roosters have personalities?

El Rosario is a town that Baja California travelers know and appreciate because it offers refuge to weary travelers in the middle of desert cactus and sagebrush. Mama Espinoza's Restaurant is a welcome haven. On our trip down the peninsula we stopped for breakfast in her restaurant which offered a delicious meal. On a trip to the outside restroom, I heard a rooster crow "Cocka doodle doo" over and over again. I stopped, looked around but couldn't see the rooster. Each time I headed toward the restroom, it crowed, but when I turned to find it, it stopped. I still didn't see it. I looked everywhere. It didn't crow while I looked, but when I walked away it would crow again. Finally, I decided the sound came from the only big tree in the yard. I looked up. There was a big black rooster happily sitting on a branch. When I held my camera toward it to take a picture, it scooted to another branch so I couldn't see it through the lens. I'm not a farm girl, so I don't know. Do roosters have personalities? Are roosters that smart? It knew I had been looking for it, so it teased me by being quiet when I looked and then it knew I wanted a picture, so it prevented me from getting it. I didn't even know roosters could climb trees or live in them, for that matter.

Why is a hog popular in Rosarito?

The largest hog I've ever seen lives in a yard on the main street in Rosarito. It must weigh hundreds of pounds. It eats 10 dozen tortillas a day as well as anything else it desires. When I observed the hog, it was trying to devour a plastic bag along with the tortillas it was eating. It's a Mexican hog with a personality because it's known in town for leading his inebriated owner home after late night escapades at the neighborhood bars. This hog actually supports and guides his owner during the late walk so that he can arrive home safely without incident.

What does it mean when someone says they're going "to pet the whales"?

During the months of December and January, gray whales migrate from Alaska to Baja California del Sur, leaving the cold waters to find warm Baja lagoons. They return north to Alaska in April either pregnant or with their babies. 15,000 whales pass through the West Coast of the Pacific for this three-month migration. They can be observed traveling south all along the coastline. When they arrive in the warm Baja California del Sur waters, they mate or they return to have babies in the same bay in which they conceived the year before. The gestation period of the whales is 12 months.

When someone says they're going to pet the whales, they mean they're going to travel south to view the whales in a *panga* on the bay in which the whales are swimming. The whales may come up to a boat and allow the passengers to pet them, but they are mostly busy giving birth, mating or training their young. A mother whale will feed her baby 200 liters of milk a day.

When they mate, a young whale will be on the bottom to stabilize the female, while an older male whale will be on top of the sandwiched female. The one on top becomes the father, while the one on the bottom learns how to do it. They weigh several tons and look rather like gigantic streamlined sea dragons. They'll roll over and over in the water, flipping their tails when they dive under, or they stick their heads up out of the water in order to breathe. Every three to five minutes they surface for air. The older ones are covered with barnacles. They're harmless creatures and often attract playful dolphins who travel with them.

The Mexican government protects these animals much like endangered species by allowing only certain guide boats to enter the bay with tourists. Strict rules are obeyed so only those who will not harm the whales will be allowed near. It's important to make lodging arrangements before traveling down to Guerrero Negro or San Ignacio to see them because many tourists go to "pet the whales" during their short visit to the Baja California del Sur waters.

Note: for lodging and tour information E-mail questions to this address: whales@balandra.uabcs.mx or call Baja Safaris in Guerrero Negro at 7-00-25 or 7-04-81 or call Motel Posada de Don Vicente at 702-88.

Are whale tours available in Ensenada?

Yes. The Science Museum of Ensenada offers informative eco-tours to view the whales by the **Todos Santos Islands** in the **Bay of Ensenada** during the months from December to March. Call (011-52)-61-78-8991 or
E-mail: museu_en@bufadora.astrosen.unam.mx or check out their website: http://www.astrosen.mx/museu_en

What is the significance of the sea turtles of Baja California?

The rare black sea turtles have used the Gulf of California, particularly Bahía de Los Angeles which lies on the Sea of Cortez in Baja California, Mexico, as a prime feeding and nursery area for years. By 1980 the population of these turtles fell off so much they are now protected by the government as an endangered species. Their meat, leather products and oil are so desirable that poachers have created a lucrative black market for them. A biologist in Bahía de Los Angeles has started a project that studies the habits of these turtles by tracking them with a tag or radio transmitter that reveals their migration habits. It's possible on the Internet to follow the turtles as they travel across the Pacific Ocean. See http://www.turtles.org/adelta.htm. Adelita is the first turtle to be tracked in this manner. She proved the theory that turtles of Baja actually travel across the Pacific Ocean for 12,000 kilometers to nest on beaches in Japan. Adelita's fate is unknown because she disappeared after her long trek, but other turtles will be sent off so more research can be accomplished. When I visited Bahía de Los Angeles they were about to release another turtle to track. I met the director of the Bahía de Los Angeles project, Antonio Resendiz. He has a research center that tourists may visit. He is willing to answer questions about his research project, which is a joint endeavor between the University of Arizona and Centro Regional de Investigaciones Pesqueras-Ensenada, Baja California. They want to answer such questions as: What do the turtles eat? Where and how far do they travel? Where do they congregate? They encourage classrooms to follow their studies and would like to have individuals join in their research teams during summer months. Check the following site for more information: http://www.earthwatch.org/Xseminoff.html

What animals can be found at Bahía de Los Angeles?

The islands offer refuge to many resident and migratory birds such as the osprey, brown pelicans, doublecrested cormorants and frigatebirds. Royal and elegant terns, Herman's gulls, and bluefooted and brown boobies travel to feed in and around Bahía. The great blue herons will nest at the great lagoon on the south end of the bay. Mangroves exist on the Isla Coronada. Sardines use the plankton-rich waters of the Sea of Cortez as a nursery, thus attracting a variety of species of fish, water mammals and reptiles. Whales such as the fin, Byde's, humpback and orca as well as the endangered blue are found in the *Canal de Ballenas* or whale canal. The whale shark that feeds only on plankton is a wonder to behold. Some tourists will jump into the water with this harmless creature for a snapshot to later show friends how they "swam with the sharks" in the Sea of Cortez.

What advice is given to tourists to preserve this ecological wonderland?

There are more than 100 islands that have sensitive ecosystems that should be preserved. The following is an excerpt from a pamphlet distributed by the *Zona de Reserva y Refugio de Aves Migratorias y de la Fauna Silvestre Isla del Golfo de California CICESE/Ecologia*:

♦ Don't bring pets or other animals to the islands.

♦ Check your clothing and equipment carefully to avoid transporting seeds or animals to the islands.

♦ Don't remove any plants, animals, shells, or rocks from the islands and don't cut cacti or shrubs or collect wood for fires—use a stove if you need to cook.

♦ Keep to the paths—the islands' desert soil and plants are very sensitive and take years to recover.

♦ Keep your distance from sea bird and sea lion colonies. Let dolphins and whale-sharks come to you. Don't pursue them.

- Help keep the islands clean—remove your garbage and, if possible, any you find.

- Go to the bathroom at the water's edge, far from bathing or disembarking areas. Carefully burn or pack out your toilet paper or use a natural alternative. Organic waste takes a long time to decompose in the desert environment.

- Find out about minimum-impact tourism and camping techniques and apply them.

Additional descriptions of the harm that can be done to the animals are as follows:

> Marine mammals, sea turtles, fish and birds also become trapped, strangled or suffocated by netting, fishing line, plastic bags, six-pack holders and other trash discarded carelessly in the bay or on the islands. The osprey, for instance, will abandon its easily accessible nest if hikers, birdwatchers or photographers don't keep their distance. Brown pelicans fly off their nests leaving them vulnerable to the immediate attacks of ravens and gull, which destroy their eggs or kill or drive chicks to a slow death, impaled on cholla cactus.

How did the frogs get on the toll road between Rosarito and Ensenada?

These frogs are not alive. In fact, an unknown artist has drawn them in life-like green on huge rocks that sit on the side of the *Cuota* between Rosarito and Ensenada. From time to time new frogs appear to the amusement of travelers. The identity of the artist is unknown.

CHAPTER FOURTEEN

ACTIVITIES, CLUBS & ENTERTAINMENT

The fifty-year Reality Check—A List of Things to
Do by Fifty—learn to: play the guitar or piano, cook,
play tennis, (speak) another language, surf, read, take
flying lessons, travel, swim with dolphins; start
therapy, go to New Orleans and Paris, learn
celestial navigation, go to the library, floss.

—Jimmy Buffet
A Pirate Looks at Fifty

How many people visit Tijuana each month?

Approximately 2,000,000 people visit Tijuana each month.

How many people cross over the five borders into Mexico per year?

Approximately 93,000,000 people cross over the border per year. Nine years ago that figure was at 91,000,000 people. Visitors to Mexico are important!

What are the recommendations of the Secretary of Tourism concerning beach activities?

◆ Watch your children closely in beach areas.

◆ If you don't know how to swim, use a flotation device.

◆ Stay close to the shore while swimming. Some beaches have dangerous rip currents and no life guard service.

◆ Maintain beaches or other sites so they are always clean.

Where can I find white sand beaches?

◆ **The Playas** in Tijuana offers a very nice beach with clean white sand and a boardwalk.

◆ **The Rosarito Beach Hotel** offers a white sandy beach.

◆ Local residents access the **Rosarito Beach** just past the immigration office.

◆ There are many coves on which hotels or subdivisions are built.

◆ **La Fonda** has a wonderful beach.

◆ **La Misión** offers a nice public beach alongside the toll road.

♦ **Estero Beach** in Ensenada—Ensenada has marinas in town but no public beaches.

Is there horseback riding available?

Yes. Horses can be rented at the south end of the town of Rosarito. There's nothing that can compare to a moonlight ride on the beach. My Fourth of July journal reads:

> When the full moon was high in the sky shimmering across the ocean, I was fortunate enough to be on a horse riding along the sandy beach. Many people were camped along the shore with fires blazing near tents or sleeping bags. Families with little children came to spend the night in the warm summer air by the Pacific Ocean. The horses threaded between the campsites under control enough to tremble each time a fire cracker went off, but not so uncomfortable as to bolt. These magic moments in the dark with campfires burning and the moon casting enough light on the ocean to see what lay ahead, the firecrackers bursting, the people happily joining us in singing as we passed on horseback, made my Fourth of July very special. In Baja California, Mexico, I experienced a holiday that will linger in my memory as one of the best! It's funny, because the people on the beach weren't celebrating Independence Day as we were. Mexicans were just celebrating a lovely summer night.

Rosarito Back Country Tours offers daylong horseback riding. They claim to have:

♦ beautiful trails through water creeks, ranches and hills

- ultimate view experiences
- strong healthy trail horses
- ranch-style barb-b-que
- hotel pick-up

Is surfing in Northern Baja California, Mexico, worthwhile?

In the north the waves are ideal for surfing. Most surfers wear wet or dry suits because the weather and water are colder than in Baja California Sur. Surfing is possible all year round. The enthusiasts are in the water on their surfboards from dawn to dusk. My journal states:

> Our condo is on the *Libre* Road at K-38.5. It's a spectacular cove because it allows the waves to break perfectly for surfing. With my binoculars I enjoy watching the surfers wait for the right wave to break. Often there'll be twenty surfers in the water bobbing like sleek seals in their black wet or dry suits. They patiently wait on their boards until a wave breaks to challenge their sense of thrill. It may take awhile, but when the big one comes they stand up on their boards like ballet dancers, perfectly balanced and in control, to ride the crest of the wave. Surfers' proper etiquette rules must take over because they let another catch the wave or they move out of the way just in time to prevent a collision. When they ride a wave, their body forms are gracefully poised as they maneuver from side to side, riding the high swell all the way into shore. When they stop, they turn around to paddle on their stomachs to the spot where the waves crest to wait again for another big one

to break. And so it goes for hours and hours. In standing on a wave, out on their stomachs. One of the older surfers revealed that over 30 years ago he camped on the vacant lot before our condos were built in order to surf in the cove. Because it's his favorite spot, he's been surfing there ever since. Some surfers have purchased their own personal condos in order to have easy access to the cove, while others have figured out a way to enter the water on the other side of the point which shelters the cove.

Where are the best surfing locations in Northern Baja California?

- **Club Marena**—K-38.5 off the Libre Road—Condo on cove—access to the side of cove

- **Cantamar**—K-53 off the toll road— the sand dunes or Punta Santa Rosalita Hotels

- **Playa Mal Paso**—K-69 off Libre Road—lovely 2.5 mile sandy beach

- **Salsipuedes & Saldamando** Campgrounds—K-87 and 94

- **Ensenada-Bahia de Todos Santos**—Playa Hermosa

- **Estero Beach**—K-B-15

- **Punta Banda**—BCN-23

What are the requirements for bringing a boat into Mexico by sea?

The customs procedures have recently been simplified,

making it much easier for foreign boaters to enjoy the coastal beauty of Mexican waters. The Secretary of Tourism states:

> If you want to bring a touring motor boat or a sailboat more than four and a half meters long (14'-16'), into the country, you must comply with the following require-ments: Upon entering the first port in Mexico, simply present the following to the immigration office and obtain a tourist entry form for each passenger aboard, if not previously obtained from a Mexican consulate, Mexican Government Tourist Office or embassy. At customs present the following in order to obtain a Temporary Import Permit:

> ♦ vessel ownership title

> ♦ document verifying that the owner of the vessel resides in a foreign country (Tourist Entry Form).

> ♦ credit card, bond or deposit mechanisms

> ♦ an official form signed by the owner, boat's captain, or legal representative on the owner's behalf

What are the requirements for bringing a boat into Mexico by land?

Proceed to the immigration office at the border crossing and obtain a Tourist Entry Form. Proceed to customs and obtain a Temporary Vehicle Import Permit, stating on the back of said permit the same information listed and bul-leted in the above answer.

Where are marinas available for boaters?

Much of the coastline is rocky with steep cliffs, so there are few marinas. Most people moor their boats in San Diego. However, a new marina called Puerto Salina is being built between Rosarito and Ensenada on K-73 off the toll road. It will have 500 slips with full services that will accommodate vessels from 25 to 120 feet in length. Homes and condominiums are available for purchase from $150,000 and up. A slip concession, which lasts for 22 years, can be purchased for a pre-construction rate of $3.78 per linear foot. ($1,000 divided by 22 years, divided by 12 months). Short-term use is also offered.

There are marinas located at the northern harbor of Ensenada:

♦ **The Coral Hotel and Marina**—Luxury hotel with a marina advertises that it's the "first marina on Northern Baja's West Coast in Ensenada." Located on K-103 Zona Playitas, there are 600 slips and 150′ guest dock. Launch ramp is $30 per day or $15 if guest of hotel with minimum of two-night stay. Long-term or short-term slips available. Slip rates are calculated according to length of vessel. Electricity, cable TV and use of hotel's amenities included. To live aboard rates are, in addition to slip rates, $100 per month for up to two people. Additional guests are $50 per person. The following words are quoted from a Coral Hotel pamphlet: "There is a full-time dock master and 24-hour security. Laundry and showers are available as well as boat maintenance, launch ramp, fuel dock and custom clearance." For more information call: 1-800-94-MARINA or (619) 523-0064.

Note: Those who wish to avoid hefty luxury taxes will buy or sell boats at this marina using offshore funds.

♦ **Sergio's Sportfishing Center and Marina**—The marina features 30 slips complete with modern amenities and 24-hour security. "Located along the recently remodeled boardwalk, it is within convenient walking distance of Ensenada's excellent shopping, dining and night life." E-mail: sergios@telnor.net or call (011-52-61) 78-2185.

♦ **Gordo's Sportfishing** is located close to the fish market at the north end of town. Call (61) 78-35-15 for more information.

If there are so few marinas how do I get re-fueled when I travel down the coast?

Seasoned captains will carry extra fuel in a drum on board; others will transport it by land from local gas stations along the way.

If I need parts to repair my vessel, can I get them across the border?

Don't assume you have customs privileges with an Import Permit for a vessel. You must research the requirements with the Mexican consulate and Mexican customs prior to returning to Mexico with the goods in order to follow the recommended exemption procedures. Otherwise, if you get caught going through the border with boxes of boat parts, you will be fined heavily and the parts will be subject to confiscation.

Does Ensenada have a port to handle large ships?

Yes. Ensenada is a major shipping port with the largest commercial fishing fleet on the West Coast. Sportfishing is offered by many large, as well as local, enterprises. Cruise ships come and go daily. Shops, restaurants and bars cater to the cruisers although the economy is not solely dependent upon tourism.

What boat charters are reputable?

◆ **Gordo's Sportfishing**—Located in Ensenada. Call (61) 78-35-15—License, poles, boat and bait provided.

◆ **Sergio's Sportfishing**—Located in Ensenada. Call (61) 78-21-85—Charters, cruises, whale watching

◆ **Ensenada Sportfishing**—Charter, whale watching or party boats available, license, rods and box lunches. Call (61) 2-01-44 ext 623

◆ **The Old Mill Hotel**—Located in San Quintin—Fishing licenses, boats and gear available. Call (619) 474-8505

◆ **Sylvia II**—22' boat available for a short trip into the Ensenada Bay or reasonable fishing trip. Skipper Manuel Ornelas says, "Look for me at the pier or call (61) 7-8-30-17 or (61) 6-66-28 after 9 PM."

What permit is necessary for hunting?

According to the Secretary of Tourism the following are necessary:

Every hunting permit should be processed by a hunting

guide, who must be registered and authorized by the Secretary of Environment Natural Resources and Fishing. The authorized guides' list may be obtained at the office of the above-mentioned agency in the city of Mexicali. To obtain a permit you have to comply with the following:

♦ Payment for each region and type of game permit.

♦ Small size picture of hunter.

♦ Authorized guides by the Secretary of Agriculture and Hydraulic Resources (S.A.R.H.).

♦ A special permit is required when hunting dogs are used. For additional information please contact the S.A.R.H. office in Tijuana or the one in Mexicali, or the nearest Mexican consulate. Telephones: (66) 83-19-48 or (65) 52-49-86.

Note: Don't bring firearms though the border. It's a felony to carry them in Mexico.

What can I hunt?

Northern Baja California is famous for quail, mountain sheep, duck, white wing and grey dove, pheasant, black tail deer and pigeons. Don't attempt to hunt without a guide or without permits.

Where do I find the guides to get the permits?

Contact Roland Torres, an official representative of the hunting organizers of Baja California. He'll explain current requirements and will obtain legal permits and guides for all your hunting needs. Call 213-385-9311 or fax 213-385-0782.

Andrés Meling is an official, registered guide who can be reached directly by calling 011-52-61-77-09-17.

What does the Secretary of Tourism say about fishing?

"Deep-sea fishing requires a fishing license, which may be obtained at the Mexican consulate or at the Fishing Office, where you may obtain all the necessary information about restrictions and closed seasons."

Telephone numbers to call:

(213) 351-6800	(619) 231-8414
(65) 52-49-86	(66) 83-19-48
(61) 76-39-37	(657) 7-14-46

Are there restrictions I need to understand?

Yes. The *Oficinas de Pescas* in Mexico at the above phone numbers will give you the current information. To obtain information concerning the requirements about bringing a catch back across the border into the States, call the California Department of Fish and Game at (619) 237-7311.

If I obtain a license through a local fishing and tackle store, by a boat operator or by a Mexican insurance dealer, is it valid?

Yes. The fishing guide or boat operator can issue the licenses. They can be issued by the day, week or month and are required for anyone 16 years or older fishing in Mexican waters. They are not transferable and each license must be in the full legal name and address of each person on the boat.

If I want to get a fishing license before crossing the border into Mexico, is it possible?

Yes. In San Diego contact the Mexico Department of Fisheries. Call (619) 233-6956

Are there informative radio shows about fishing?

Yes. Listen to **"Let's Talk Hook-up"** on 690 AM radio, Saturdays and Sundays 6 AM to 8 AM. Freshwater and saltwater techniques, tackle and travel are topics. E-mail: hookup690@aol.com or phone (760) 941-3474.

What clubs would be good to join for outdoor adventure?

♦ **The Vagabundos Del Mar Boat and Travel Club**—Save money, travel safely and have fun throughout North America but especially in Baja California. Dues—$35 per year. Call (800) 474-2252
E-mail address: VAGS@compuserve.com

♦ **Discover Baja Travel Club**—Latest information on roads, weather, fuel and fishing with discounts. Dues—$39 per year (800) 727-2252 E-mail address: discovbaja@aol.com

What tennis clubs are available?

Baja Tennis Club in Ensenada has five professional courts, a pro shop, racket services, tennis clinics, a family club, heated pool, aqua-aerobic classes, sauna and showers, and locker rooms. Located on Ave Isla San Benito #123,

Ensenada, call for more information: (61) 76-21-13.

Tennis courts can be found at almost every private subdivision complex.

Are there any golf courses available in Baja California?

Yes. The following courses are available:

♦ **Tijuana Country Club**—Also called *Social Campestre*, it is an 18-hole golf course located on Agua Caliente in downtown Tijuana. Call (66) 81-78-51.

♦ **Real Del Mar Golf Course**—18 holes. Located on K-19.5 just north of Rosarito on hill overlooking ocean. Marriott Residence Inn available on grounds. Call (66) 31-36-70.

♦ **Bajamar**—18 holes plus three Scottish link courses set high above the Pacific Ocean.Sometimes called the "Pebble Beach" of Baja California Mexico. Located on K-77.5 on toll road between Rosarito and Ensenada. Call (615) 5-0161.

♦ **Baja Country Club**—18 holes. Located on Km-18 seven miles south of Ensenada off Highway 1. Call (61) 73-0303.

Clubs can be rented at each golf course and accommodations are available.

Where is *jai alai* played?

The *Jai Alai* Palace or **Fronton Palacio** is located in downtown Tijuana in a unique building that has become a famous landmark on Revolution and 7th Street. Games are played Friday and Saturday nights from 7-10 PM. This game is considered the fastest game in the world. It's a cross between tennis and handball. Betting is allowed. Don't miss it. Call (011-52-66) 8 5-36-87 or (619) 231-1910.

Where are the cave paintings?

There are over 100 sites with hieroglyphics on the Baja California peninsula. They represent silent communication from an early race that even the Cochimíes Indians can't explain. Some historians date the drawings to be several thousand years old. They are unique remains of a mysterious past history of a people who resided in the mountains and desert of Baja California. There are sites near the mission in San Ignacio in Baja California del Sur but the most well-known paintings are geometric figures drawn on the ceiling of a cave close to Cataviña. Take the turn-off a half mile past K-170.

What is offered at the Tijuana Cultural Center?

Located on the Paseo de Los Heroes, the **Tijuana Cultural Center** is a landmark in Tijuana. It offers a museum, exhibit halls, a Performing Arts Theater, bookstore and restaurant. Mexican art is exhibited and historical artifacts displayed. Various performances are presented throughout the year. One of the most popular is the "Flying Pole Dance" performed by the Totonac Indian troupe during the summer months in the outdoor garden. It's a spectacular performance with flute and drum accompaniment where they spin themselves out into the air from a tree trunk hooked together four at a time with flute and drum accompaniment. Call (66) 84-1111 for more information.

Does Ensenada have a city theater?

Yes. Musicals, ballets and plays are presented in the *Teatro de La Ciudad*, or City Theater located between Loyola and Reforma. Call 77-0392 for current schedule of events.

How can I learn about future events or activities in the area?

Call Armando Carrasco at **Too Much Fun Promotions** (011-52-661-2-25-25).

Where are rock concerts performed?

Rock concerts are performed from May through September at **Mexitlan** located on Calle 2 and Avenida Ocampo in Tijuana. Call (66) 38-4101.

Where are dog races held?

The **Caliente Racetrack** in Tijuana off Boulevard Agua Caliente offers greyhound races every night and at 2 PM on Saturdays and Sundays. Call (011-52-66) 337300 ext 4207.

Is gambling allowed?

US horse racing and professional sports betting are popular in Tijuana. Phone (800) 745-2252 for more information. Casino gambling is currently against the law in Mexico; however, it's been rumored that it will become legal soon. Rosarito is a possible location for a casino.

Is there a wax museum?

Yes. The *Museo de Cera de Tijuana*, or the wax museum, is famous. Off Revolution Avenue at Calle 1, this museum houses famous figures in wax. Call (66) 88-2478 for more information.

Where are amusement parks?

In Tijuana *Mundo Divertido* or **Fun World** is located at the corner of Paseo de Los Heroes and Jose Ma.Velasco. It offers rides for a small fee. Call (66) 34-3234.

During the summer, a temporary amusement park is set up at the north end of Rosarito. It's removed during the winter months.

Where can I take the family for food and fun?

Epocas family fun center in Ensenada offers a restaurant, go karts, ping-pong, billiards, ice cream parlor, video games, etc. for all ages. Located on Calle Delante #314. Call (61) 77-2420.

Where are the bullfights?

There are two bullfight rings in Tijuana. The older one is located in downtown Tijuana on Agua Caliente, while the newer ring is located in Las Playas. This sport is considered by the Mexican culture as an art form symbolic of man interacting with animal. The matador trains to fine tune his skill for years, just as any performer would prepare for the theater. When he steps out to meet the bull, his life is on the line. His graceful movements are applauded and his courage revered. Mexicans do not consider a bullfight to be a brutal slaughtering of an animal. In fact, there are times when the bull is given a *corrida*, which spares his life. Sometimes the bull may even win the competition. Bullfights are an art form that's deeply rooted in Mexican history and culture. Don't expect it to change.

Are there any arts and crafts fairs?

There's an arts and crafts fair during a weekend in August in Ensenada. Food, wine tasting, demonstrations, sales by local artists and musical entertainment are offered. For information call (800) 310-9687.

Can I ride in a horse-drawn carriage?

Yes. Ensenada offers a ride in an open horse-drawn carriage on Costero Blvd. It's called a *calandrias*.

What activities are offered during the Ensenada wine festival?

The wine festival, generally in August, has many activities and lasts for ten days. It starts with a visit to some of the wineries with tours guided by the winemaker. Complimentary snacks and wineglasses are given to those who attend. The wine competition, in which a professional panel judges wines from Baja California and other regions, takes place followed by a formal dinner with an auction of wine and art in addition to the awards ceremony. A golf tournament at the Baja Country Club with lunch and wine tasting of Baja California wines occurs the next day. In the evening the golf awards ceremony takes place during a dinner made of ingredients and wines from Baja California. A winery will host a concert of music at sunset on the following two evenings. A piano concert from the romantic era with wine tasting and hors d'oeuvres is offered at another winery the next evening. The next night celebrates the crush of the grapes with dinner, dancing and fireworks. The final evening is the folkfest of San Tomas. Art, games, music, Mexican food and house wines are offered at this street fair outside the winery. **The Vintners' Association** plans all activities. Call (011-52-617) 8-3146 for specific current information.

What is the *Fiesta Colores de Vendimia?*

The **L.A. Cetto winery** located between Ensenada and Tecate in the Calafia Valley celebrates, as part of the wine festival, the harvest of grapes with fireworks, dinner and starlight dancing outside in the vineyard. It begins during the day with a mariachi mass, which blesses the harvest. Then grapes are crushed during a grape-stomping contest. An art show is also offered. Tickets are $75 and must be purchased in advanced. Call (011-52-66) 853031.

What activities are scheduled during the Seafood Fair in Ensenada?

The Seafood Fair is an international culinary event that has taken place in Ensenada in mid-September of each year for the last twenty years. Organized by CANTRAC Chamber of Restaurants, it takes place on the grounds of a local hotel. Live entertainment, raffles, a waiters' footrace, a *Senorita Gastronomia* pageant and a special *Mandil de Oro* (gold apron) cooking contest for couples who prepare traditional Mexican dishes of *ceviche* and *bacalao* (salted codfish). Quoted from the newspaper, *South of the Border*, written by Connie Ellig:

> . . . top chefs from restaurants on both sides of the border engaged in a culinary battle for trophies and honor while preparing their best seafood dishes in six different categories: cold and hot fin fish, cold and hot shellfish, artistic showpiece creation and Baja California Dish. The competition was judged by Chefs de Cuisine Association of San Diego who evaluated the various entries on bases of presentation, practicality and taste. Shrimp brochettes, seafood gumbo, fettuccine with mussels, abalone sausage, scallop *ceviche*, and clams au gratin were merely a few of the delicacies from the deep sampled by more than 1,500 visitors at the Ensenada International Seafood Fair on Sunday. . . .

What is the *Riviera Del Pacifico*?

It is an elegant historical building in Ensenada that was originally used as a gambling casino in the 1930s. It is now a cultural center and museum with lovely gardens. Located on Blvd. Costero in the center of town, it's a must to visit in Ensenada.

Where is the open-air fish market located in Ensenada?

This market is located on the waterside of the main street of Ensenada on Costero Blvd. Often called *Mercado Negro*, or the **Black Market**, it's a fascinating market to visit. Every fish imaginable is on display. Halibut, tuna, shrimp, octopus or clams are just a few of the fresh catch offered to purchase. Grab a fish taco at one of the booths outside the market and take your time deciding which fish you will fix for dinner that night. Be careful, the eye of the fish may cause you to think it's watching you as you have the entire body wrapped up for the trip home.

What is *The Window of the Sea*?

At the back of the Fish Market, there is a boardwalk called The Window of the Sea. View the bay with its many boats and sea life, or take a short cruise on a sightseeing boat.

What is *The Three Head's Park*?

Ensenada has a *Plaza Civica* or park at the corner of Blvd. Costero & Macheros. It hosts giant golden busts of Mexican heroes, Benito Juarez, Miguel Hidalgo, and Venustiano Carranza.

Does Ensenada have swap meets?

Yes. *Los Globos* outdoor swap meet on Calle 9, three blocks east of Reforma, offers many treasures for sale at bargain prices.

What is *Las Cigüeñas*?

In Ensenada, once a year the ladies offer a costume party for the community for which they sell tickets to benefit the DIF charity. (See page 139.) Seven or eight hundred women attend whether old or young or rich or poor. No men are invited. Each woman wears an elaborate costume, which could include a headdress and train made of the finest materials. Great care and elaborate expense goes into each costume. A queen and two princesses are elected to reign over the next year's celebration. A parade of costumes takes place while live music, a band and dancing goes on into the early morning. *Las Cigüeñas*, meaning **The Stork**, is the name of this event.

What is *Carnaval*?

Carnaval, held in Ensenada each year, is similar to Mardi Gras in New Orleans, but it's geared more for families. It takes place the last week before the beginning of Lent. Music, dancing, poetry readings, a bonfire to rid the town of bad humor, costume parties and the **Night of the Oppressed Husbands** are only a few of the activities that take place. The selection of a king and queen begins in January and continues until the formal black-tie coronation takes place on the last Saturday night of Carnaval. Parades, complete with floats and elaborate costumes, are the highlights of the celebration. For children there are clowns, balloons, puppet shows and magicians.

What is the Tecate SCORE Baja 1000?

It's a desert race for cars, trucks, motorcycles and ATVs

which transverse 1000 miles of desert between Santo Tomas and La Paz. All the pre-race activities occur in Ensenada as they have for 31 years. It's televised internationally and brings over 250 racers from the USA, Canada, Europe and Japan along with a large contingent of racers from Mexico. "We have had tremendous cooperation from both states in Baja California, as well as the officials from Ensenada, Santo Tomas, and La Paz . . . in the true spirit of Baja," adds Sal Fish, CEO of SCORE. "We are visitors in their country and we need all of their assistance to continue the legend of the Tecate SCORE Baja 1000."

This group has also given back to Mexico by presenting the Flying Samaritan charity organization a check for nearly $2000. It will go a long way to help the poor who need medical assistance in Mexico. Thank you, racers of the Baja 1000, for the generous contribution.

What is the Newport Yacht Race?

The Newport Yacht Race starts in Newport, California, and ends in Ensenada. Sailors from various areas participate in the race. The boats are decorated, elaborate feasts are prepared and singing celebrations occur. The spinnakers are lovely as they approach the Ensenada harbor.

What clubs are available to join in the Rosarito area?

There are many clubs offering American residents membership in the Rosarito area:

◆ **The United Society of Baja California**—This club sends a newsletter, *The Communicator,* to its members that contains a calendar of events for the upcoming month. It includes activities and dates of its board meetings, fund raising events, bridge and book club meetings as well as activities of other groups in the area. Bill McClendon is the current president. Call (661) 2-3533 for more information or send $12 to: USBC, PO Box 439030, San Ysidro, California 92143.

◆ **Thursday Ladies Club**—These ladies play cards at designated homes or local restaurants at least once a week. They spend at least one day at the races in August. Sounds like a popular activity since all tickets sold out early. Call (66) 31-3493 for information.

◆ **Book Club**—Call (661) 2-3850 for information. Read a book once a month to discuss with other members.

◆ **Bridge**—Observers are welcome. Beginners and brush-up class meets Wednesdays at 1 PM at Hacienda de Badu Restaurant. Duplicate, Mondays at 12:00 AM. Call Dody (661) 2-1257.

◆ **Deep Sea Fishing**—No set schedule but if interested, call Captain Phil (66) 31-3493.

◆ **Knit**—Free classes. Knitters of all levels welcomed. Call (66) 31-3896.

◆ **Golf**—call Bud (66) 31-3171.

◆ **Rosarito Theater Guild**—If you have singing or acting ability or if you're just interested in the arts, this club is for you. Call John Finch (661) 31-3463 for more information. It is rumored that a play reading group is meeting the third Tuesday of each month at noon. The location will be at La Masia Restaurant. Some recent plays that have been performed are *Said the Spider to the Spy*, *South Pacific* and the *Odd Couple*.

♦ **Diamond Chorale**—This is a group of singers who would love to have you join them. Contact Mavourneen at (66) 31-3428.

♦ **Adult Tapping Class**—For fun and exercise. Cost: $10. Call Trudy for schedule (661) 2-0016.

♦ **AA & Al-Anon**—Join the AA for breakfast on Thursdays at 9 at Naty's. Meetings are at 10 AM Monday, Thursday and Sunday or at 6 PM Tuesday, Wednesday and Friday. There are no fees or dues. Call (661) 2-1444 for more information.

♦ **The Umbrella Association**—Local legal homeowners' association meets on the second Monday of each month at 8:30 AM at La Cazu Mole Restaurant. This group seeks to work with residents and government to resolve mutual concerns. Call for more information: (66) 31-3631.

What charity organizations are available to join?

♦ **Baja Animal Sanctuary**—The following is quoted from an advertising pamphlet:

The Baja Animal Sanctuary, A.C., was founded in 1997. Our goal is to rescue abandoned and abused animals, place them in a safe environment, attend their health needs and put them up for adoption. We care for the unfortunate animals that have no homes, no food and no one to love them. Many are starving and ill and all of them are scared and lonely. If you have seen these animals on the streets and wished that you could help

in some way . . . NOW YOU CAN! Join with us and MAKE A DIFFERENCE! We need volunteers to come to the Sanctuary and work with the animals; we need loving families to adopt a dog or cat and give them a second chance at life AND we need financial support. Even a small amount will help us continue to care for the many animals whose lives depend on us. Educating the public regarding proper care of animals is one of our main concerns. Dogs and cats that are loved and cared for will never need our help. PLEASE TREAT ALL ANIMALS WITH RESPECT. If you can help, please call 31-32-49.
Website: http://home.earthlink.net/~bajsanctuary/

♦ **Casa de Paz** provides quality physical, emotional and spiritual care for Mexican citizens who have no family or are living at the poverty level of income and who are terminally ill. The following are offered as hospice support:
> On-going support and education for loved ones.
> Effective pain control and symptom management.
> Burial services.

Volunteers and financial donations are needed.
Contact 011-52-66-31-36-28 or
E-mail: Casadepazmexico@hotmail.com

♦ **Cruz Roja Mexicana**—In Baja the government sets up medical clinics in the towns, but it's the local people who have to support and upgrade them. Volunteers are invited to join this group of individuals who are willing to support the local Red Cross which provides the hospital and ambulance service for the Rosarito area. This local delegation provides the sole funding for this important service. Dues, contributions and fund raising activities have been a source of funding since 1974. Members help with the thrift shop, fashion shows or auctions. The hospital is staffed full-time with doctors and nurses who perform all types of emergency medical services as well as minor surgeries and newborn deliveries. The Red Cross provides the only ambulance service in town. Dues are $12.50 yearly. Send a check to: Mexican Red Cross PO Box 433220 San Ysidro, CA 92143-3220.

♦ **The Flying Samaritans**—Free medical-dental help is offered to the needy people of Rosarito through this group of volunteers who opened a clinic on June 8, 1996, at #7 Calle Del Aberto. The clinic, open only on Saturday, offers treatment, care and medications for general ailments. Up to 72 patients are helped per day. Doctors, dentists, nurses, translators, pilots and support personnel all offer their services freely to help people who would otherwise go untreated, such as children who may need to be referred to Shriner's Hospital in Los Angeles or old people who need medication for high blood pressure. So much more is needed. Rent for the building is $300 per month. Medications, supplies and time are needed from volunteers. The Flying Samaritans offers a tangible way for you to contribute to a worthy cause. Dues are $25 per year. Call B.J. Carpenter (661) 2-06-31 for more information.

Mama Espinoza's book entitled *Reflections* describes the unique birth of this philanthropic group. In the following excerpt this remarkable lady refers to those who were in an airplane in distress that landed on a mesa in November of 1961, a time of devastating drought that plunged her little pueblo of El Rosario into economic disaster. She sent her husband to retrieve the stranded five on the desolate mesa, fixed them a meal and explained that the hospital had been abandoned and there were no medical supplies:

> I told them I was so embarrassed and sorry that I could
> not do anything better for them. I told them of the
> poverty of the *pueblo*, about the drought which had
> ruined the harvest and crops, and how the cattle were
> dying for the lack of rain. . . I planted a seed, yes, I did,
> for in a few weeks a letter arrived from Eileen and Polly
> Ross. They thanked the people of El Rosario for their
> help and said that fliers would come on December 6, to
> bring medicines and food. The seed has sprouted. This
> would become the beginning of the Flying Samaritans.

> They were true to their word. It was beautiful! Just like
> a big dream. Nine airplanes formed stairsteps into the
> sky. The airplanes were loaded with Christmas gifts,
> food, medicine, dry milk and clothing. A reporter of the
> San Diego Union wrote in his paper: 'Over 100 children
> and youngsters were standing astonished, waiting for
> the arrival and for sure what they were going to
> receive.' Dr. Dale Hoyt in his Bonanza came. Dr. Hoyt
> quickly noticed people needed medical attention, so
> being a man of action, he came to me and opened his
> bag and said: 'I will see anyone who would like my
> help.' Quickly, I found some sheets for privacy and
> they used my kitchen table as an examination table. Dr.
> Hoyt was soon out of supplies but promised to be back
> in two weeks. When Dr. Hoyt opened his big black bag,
> the Flying Samaritans began. That was the 6th of
> December of 1961. Within the year, Mexicans south of
> El Rosario began making long trips to come and be
> seen by the Flying Samaritans . . . it was a pilgrimage,
> how they arrived and camped in the arroyo bottom,
> waiting to be seen by the doctors.

Note: For a copy of this historical book, phone (011-52-61) 76-32-16, Ensenada, B.C., Mexico.

What Mexican holidays and activities are to be remembered?

What is a *Quincenera*?

A *Quincenera* is a *fiesta* or celebration of a young woman who is transitioning from childhood to adulthood at age 15. It's a celebration that can cost as much as a wedding in the United States. The young lady wears a dress like a wedding dress while those in attendance dress formally. A church mass, a meal, photographs and dancing are offered to family and friends of the young woman. It's a *fiesta* that may last into the early morning hours of the next day.

What is *The Day of the Dead*?

November 2nd or *El Día de Todos Santos* is celebrated as **The Day of the Dead**. Families visit the gravesites of loved ones for a picnic. The gravesite is cleaned, flowers are placed and favorite food of the departed is eaten. Discussions with the departed or special memories of that person are shared. At home, a shrine is created for the dead where items they cherished as well as a picture of the loved one may be displayed. A special loaf of bread, called *pan de muerto* or "bread of death", is served to family members. The person to bite into a piece with a tiny toy skeleton will receive good luck. Coffins with skeletons that rise out of them are given as toys to the children and candied skulls personalized with names on them are eaten as treats. A crown made out of paper maché is made for each person in the family who died.

It is not a morbid time where everyone is sad. Instead, it's a joyous remembrance of those who are no longer living. It's a way of honoring the dead and celebrating life. Tourists often feel Mexicans are obsessed with the concept of death, especially when they observe shrines on the roadside marking the place where a loved one died, or in the yard of a home where the person lived. Instead, those who still live are actually honoring the dead with a message of, "We remember and love you. We honor you." The shrine is placed to catch the spirit where it was last alive. The living can talk with the spirit of the dead person at the shrine in order to share their feelings in an outpouring of catharsis. The Day of the Dead is a joyous way of uniting the family, both the living and the dead.

What is the *Day of Our Lady of Guadalupe*?

When Mexicans celebrate the Christmas season, December 12th rates among the most commemorative religious days. It is the **Day of Our Lady of Guadalupe**. When the Spanish conquerors destroyed the Aztec statues of gods and goddesses, there was an attempt to make the Indians forget their beloved goddess. However, in 1531 a miracle occurred to an Indian named Juan Diego. He claimed the Virgin Mary appeared requesting that a church be built and dedicated to her at the very spot on a hill known as Tepeyac where the goddess' statue had stood. When he told Bishop Juan de Zumarraga this story, the bishop demanded proof. Juan returned to the hill where the Virgin Mary appeared to him again. She told him to gather roses from the barren ground and to return to the Bishop with them. He placed the beautiful roses, which were obviously not from the area, into his blanket and returned to the Bishop. When he presented them to the Bishop, his blanket fell open. The flowers spilled onto the floor and to the amazement of all, a portrait of the Virgin Mary was embedded on the inside of the blanket. The church was built in honor of Our Lady of Guadalupe. Thousands visit the shrine each December. The portrait on the blanket is now displayed in the Basilica in Mexico City. It represents an important miracle in the country of Mexico. Celebrations or *fiestas* occur on this day all over Mexico. A big procession with costumes, floats and mini dramas takes place on the way to the Cathedral of Our Lady of Guadalupe.

What is a *posada*?

December 16th marks the beginning of nine *posadas*, which will occur each night before Christmas. They are religious re-enactments of the experience of Mary and Joseph as they looked for an inn to find rest. The word *posada* means a "resting place" or an "inn". The number nine symbolizes the nine months of Mary's pregnancy. Each night a procession of people wearing costumes carry lighted candles, singing a song asking for refuge as they go through the local neighborhood to nine houses. A group inside each house they pass sings a retort to continue on. "There is no room. Keep on going." Finally they come to a home that allows them to enter. At this home there are more songs, hot chocolate or punch, and a *piñata* to break, spilling out candies, fruits, peanuts, etc. Children participate in these events, sometimes playing the roles of Mary and Joseph, shepherds and the three kings.

What are *Las Pastorelas*?

These are shepherds' plays or dramas which occur throughout the holiday season to represent the shepherds attempt to follow the star of Bethlehem. Angels and devils play a role in helping or hindering the quest. Children look forward to these portrayals because they get to wear colorful costumes and participate in the festivities.

What is *La Noche Buena*?

La Noche Buena is December 24th or **Christmas Eve**. Families gather to celebrate the birth of Jesus. A rustic or elaborate nativity scene is filled with figures of angels, shepherds, livestock, devils, the three kings, Mary and Joseph with a crib in a manger. The star illuminates the scene. Each night of the season the shepherds and kings are moved closer to the manger until this night when they finally arrive. The youngest child of the family brings in the figurine of the baby Jesus for each to kiss before it is placed in the empty crib. A celebration with food and drink continues into the early morning.

What is *El Día de Los Santos Inocentes*?

El Día de Los Santos Inocentes or **The Day of Holy Innocents**, is much like our April Fool's Day where jokes and pranks may be played on an unsuspecting innocent. December 28th represents the day King Herod ordered the slaughter of the male infants. A victim who falls prey to a prank is required to give a little gift to the prankster.

What is *Las Días de Los Reyes Magos*?

Días de Los Reyes Magos is Epiphany or **Three Kings Day**. On January 6th the "Magi" leave gifts in shoes set out on the front porch for the children. They represent the gifts the three kings brought to the baby Jesus.

What is the feast day of *Our Lady of the Candelaria*?

February 2nd signifies the fortieth day after Christ was born and is called **Candlemas**. It is the official last day of the Christmas season. The person who received a bean or little doll in the cake that was served on the Three Kings Day gives a party.

Christmas is an ongoing family affair that incorporates religious training with celebrations. The excitement and joy in the children for the parades, dramas and parties is truly delightful. Santa Claus and elaborate gift exchange are not a part of it. It would be wise to gain understanding of the Mexican-style holiday instead of imposing United States' expectations upon the people.

The calendar dates listed below indicate national Mexican holidays as well as yearly Baja California events. Baja California towns observe them by closing government businesses and in some cases the local stores. It's helpful to be aware of these dates so that you can make plans to participate in the *fiestas* and celebrations. Also, you can plan to avoid crossing the border or going into town when traffic congestion is at its worst. The events that are marked in **bold** are local yearly activities that impact the community with an influx of visitors and tourists.

January
1—New Year's day celebration
6—Three Kings Day. Presents are exchanged.

February
5—Constitution Day (Independence Day)
World Surfing Championships in Ensenada
Mardi Gras Parades in Ensenada
National Mountain Bike Race at Real Del Mar
Shells and Wine Festival at Santo Tomas Cultural Center

March
21—Birthday of Benito Juarez, a famous past
Mexican president. First day of spring

April
California Racing Series off-road rally in Ensenada
Semana Santa—Holy Week and Easter
Rosarito to Ensenada bicycle race
Estero Beach Stadium off-road races

May
1—Mexican national holiday like Labor Day (day of rest)
5—*Cinco de Mayo*—celebrates the defeat of France
     in 1862—parade
Mother's Day—celebrated highly
Tecate-Ensenada Bike Ride

June
1—Navy Day—Mexican holiday
SCORE Baja 500 off-road race—starts in Ensenada

Estero Beach Volleyball Tournament

July
4—Cruz Roja Celebration next to René's in Rosarito
Baja Promotional International jet-ski races in Ensenada

August
1-2— Piñata Parade—on Paseo de Los Heroes in Tijuana
**Books and Reading Fair—Ensenada Jazz Outdoor Concert
& Festival in courtyard of Tijuana Cultural Center
Wine Festival—Ensenada**
Caesar Salad Festival in Tijuana on Revolution Avenue
**Todos Santos Regata—Hobie Cats Race—Ensenada
Cruz Roja Fashion Show—Rosarito**

September
8—Celebrates Baja's first mission
Ensenada seafood fair
15-16—Independence Day—Celebrates Mexican revolt
against Spanish—parade
**Folklorico International Competition in Ensenada
Rosarito to Ensenada bicycle race
Estero Beach Stadium Races off-road races**

October
**Southwestern Country Club Marlin Tournament
in Ensenada**
12—Columbus Day—honors the discovery of the Americas
**Fiestas De Las Fronteras at Calafia Hotel
Ensenada Grand Prix Street Race
Juan Hussong International Chili Cookoff in Ensenada
Halloween Party for Cruz Roja in Rosarito**

November
1-2— All Saints' Day & All Souls' Day—picnic at the grave
of family member
SCORE—Baja 1000 Off-road Race

20—Revolution Day marking the Mexican Civil War of 1910—parade

December
Black and White Dinner Dance for Cruz Roja Charity
Christmas Surfing Tournament at Playa San Miguel
California Gray Whale Watching Tours begin and continue through March
12— Day of the Virgin of Guadalupe—7 days of the flag
16— Day to celebrate Joseph and Mary's search for shelter in Bethlehem
25— Christmas—*Navidad*

American holidays, especially three-day weekends, cause unusual traffic back-up at the border with Americans returning to the US.

Is it true that famous people visit Rosarito?

Rosarito Beach, once a quiet little fishing village, became popular in the 1920s, particularly among rich and famous Americans, many of whom were Hollywood stars wanting to play in privacy. The Rosarito Beach Hotel, still located on the Main Street of Rosarito, was the chosen hot spot. Marilyn Monroe, Clark Gable and Vincent Price are examples of stars who chose to visit this town.

It's common today to see popular Hollywood people, particularly when a new movie is being produced. This is especially true since the Twentieth Century Fox Studio has been built on the Pacific coast just south of town. The Titanic production brought many famous faces to town. Each time a new movie is produced, an entirely new set of famous stars appear.

Another group of talented people are those who were famous in the past and have retired in Palm Springs where it's hot in the summer. Where do they go for mild weather? They choose Rosarito, of course! Many prefer a low profile, so they'll go to the local establishments that are not necessarily known to the typical tourist. They wish to maintain their privacy, so if I share the names of the local places they visit, please leave them alone. If they want to be noticed, they'll get up to sing or dance or will in some way let you know who they are. One singer sang his heart out the other night in a local establishment, not as an entertainer, but as an average customer. His manner and voice were so professional, we knew we were the recipients of a special treat.

One celebrity expressed the common feeling of well-known people when she said, "I want to be accepted for who I am, not because I'm famous. Just consider me another child of God."

What is a *mariachi* band?

Passionate, romantic, rhythmic are adjectives used to describe Mexican music. It offers inherent pleasure, which mirrors the soul of the culture. A *mariachi* band plays guitars, violins and trumpets. These strolling bands can be found in restaurants such as those in Puerto Nuevo. They'll entertain while you dine for $3-$5. They can also be hired for party entertainment or as Aldolfo Kim explains, "Whenever I make my wife angry, I'll go into Tijuana and hire a *mariachi* band to sing under her window. If she turns her light on, I know she's not angry anymore. However, if the light stays off, I'm still in the doghouse."

What nightspots are recommended?

The following nightspots are popular among the local inhabitants of the Rosarito area and are rarely advertised. Don't dress up. They are not fancy. Expect to pay cash, as no credit cards are accepted.

♦ **La Gondola**—This nightclub has the quaint, funky charm of Mexico. It is not fancy. Paco, the owner, plays the guitar and sings romantic ballads. He doesn't mind if the patrons play the drum and tambourine while he sings. On Wednesday and Thursday nights Miguel De Hoyos plays classical guitar with the expertise of a master. He mesmerizes the patrons with his music, which comes straight from his soul. Ask him if you can purchase his new CD, which is a marvelous treasure. To find the Gondola, turn west off the main street when you see the Thrifty Ice Cream sign. Go one block to a building on the right side of the street. The Gondola is located upstairs. My journal describes Miguel's talent:

> The evening was spent listening to Miguel De Hoyos playing his guitar. He's a master guitarist from Monterrey, Mexico, whose fingers manipulate the strings to make magical music. He plays from his soul such pieces as, "Bolero" or "Lara's Theme" in a mesmerizing crescendo of tunes. What a treat to hear such talent in an intimate local bar, rather than in a concert hall with thousands of listeners, which is where he's destined to play in the future.

♦ **René's**—This is the place for playing pool or darts with the local people. It has a wonderful dance floor, so if you also like to dance to Mexican music, this is the place to go. The dancing doesn't begin until after midnight, so don't expect to be an early bird. It's located south of town just after crossing the little bridge. By the way, it's a sports bar and restaurant as well. It's an historical spot dating back the 1920s.

♦ **Costa Baja**—This place offers free dinners on Wednesday nights and music Thursday, Friday and Saturday nights. It's a fun little joint located on K-36 on the Libre Road south of Rosarito. You'll see a picture of the Titanic hanging on the wall, signed by the entire cast of the award-winning movie. Don't read the signs behind the bar if you don't want to learn off-color Spanish phrases.

♦ **Bahia Cantiles**—This wonderful place has been called the Mexican version of the Cheers Bar. It is so popular that even a fire that burned the building to the ground didn't prevent it from continuing on in fine fashion. The owners simply moved the business into their home, located behind the original building. They now live in a trailer next door. Rosa, the female owner, says she's happy because her house is now finished. Dan, the male owner, sings Wednesday through Sunday, while a live band plays on the weekend nights. Salsa, rock and roll and romantic songs are offered.

Note: Happy hour is Monday through Friday from 4 PM to 6 PM. Drinks are two for the price of one and beers are $1. Appetizers are half price. For example: Quesadillas are $1.25 while steamed clams are $2.25. Located at K- 43 on the Libre road, this is a place to visit.

♦ **Carlos Country**—Located just after the checkpoint on the *Libre* Road south of Rosarito, it offers the best prices for drinks in town. The live band called The Guayson plays *"oldies but goodies"* as well as romantic Mexican music that is good for dancing. Go on a Thursday night when they serve a steak dinner for a reasonable price. It's a favorite place for the local residents to gather for fun.

◆ **La Masia**—This is a restaurant and bar at the La Quinta del Mar, K-25.5 in downtown Rosarito. "Come to enjoy our Thursday traditional special" is an offer they make for reasonably priced continental cuisine.
Call (011-52-661) 3-0290 for more information.

CHAPTER FIFTEEN

PURCHASING PROPERTY IN MEXICO

**Some men have thousands of reasons why they
cannot do what they want to, when all they
need is one reason why they can.**
—Dr. Willis R. Whitney

Is the process of purchasing a property in Baja California different from that in the United States?

In some respects the process differs but the end result is the same. If a buyer wants to buy and a seller wants to sell, a transfer of property will occur. Legal documents are necessary and filing the transaction with the government is expected. How this transfer occurs requires knowledge and guidance. Just as in any purchase, a buyer needs to be alert and aware of hazards that could cost money and cause inconvenience. I recommend obtaining a professional real estate agent or knowledgeable Mexican lawyer who can be trusted as a guide through the purchase procedure.

There are four ways for a foreigner to hold property in Mexico.

1. *Fideicomiso* or Mexican Bank Trust

This method of ownership was created in 1971 to encourage foreign investments along the popular coastlines. These investments had been prohibited by the Mexican Constitution of 1917. Direct titles to land within 60 miles of the border and 30 miles of coastline (a restricted zone) are not given to foreigners. A bank trust allows non-Mexicans to purchase indirectly by setting up a property trust that is recorded in a Mexican trustee's name in a Mexican bank's trust department. It must be officially created through an authorized Mexican bank. A seller will convey title to the bank, which then acts as the trustee for the foreigner buyer. The purchaser is the sole beneficiary of this trust. It is he who has the ownership rights to the property, not the bank. When he chooses to sell, he will be the sole recipient of the funds, not the bank. In the meantime, he may improve, rent or live on the property as he sees fit. It is actually an advantage to have a bank trust. The bank acts as a protection against title disputes and hence is a type of insurance. It is against the law for a trustee to transfer the property or the beneficiary rights without legal permission of the beneficiary.

What does the bank trust cost?

The bank receives payment from the beneficiary to set up a trust. It then receives a yearly fee to maintain the trust. Currently the set-up fee is determined by a percentage of the purchase price and ranges between $350 to $500 per year thereafter, depending on the bank.

How long does the bank trust last?

These trusts endure for 50 years at which time they can be renewed. The property does not have to revert back to a Mexican national. In the meantime, if the property sells to another foreigner, that person simply assumes the balance of the bank term and the legal documents are made to place the bank trust in the new buyer's name with his or her beneficiary. A Mexican national purchaser can cancel the trust and take fee simple title.

What is the procedure for setting up a bank trust?

♦ Application is made to the Secretary of Foreign Relations for a permit to establish the trust.

♦ When a permit is received, the trustee sends instruction to notary for preparation of deed.

♦ Applicable taxes are paid.

♦ Deed is recorded in the appropriate municipality for the location of the property.

Note: While setting up the paperwork for the trust, ask your representative to negotiate a set yearly renewal fee rather than a percentage of the market value of the property. If a large appreciation occurs over the years, you will not have the fee increase as you would on a percentage basis. I predict all property in Northern Baja California,

Mexico, will indeed increase over the upcoming years unless some major catastrophe occurs.

2. Master Bank Trust

If a developer has obtained a bank trust for his subdivision or condominium project, he should have certified legal documents to verify it. It's a long legal process initially for the developer to obtain, but it acts as an assurance to the buyer that the developer has a legal right to sell and it helps the purchaser assume the balance of the term under the master trust, thus saving the purchaser money. It is wise for a purchaser to have knowledge of the developers that have and have not obtained a master trust for their development projects.

3. Mexican Land Lease

A land lease is an arrangement in which the owner collects compensation for the use of his land. In Mexico it is illegal to lease land for more than a 10-year maximum. Make certain you don't sign a lease for a longer period or your agreement will not be honored in court.

Many people lease land from a Mexican owner and don't hesitate to build expensive homes on the land. My caution is to be aware that unless stated otherwise in the contract, the landlord can terminate the lease at the end of the term. If you purchase such a property, make certain you read the original lease agreement and make a price adjustment for risk factors. Many have been successful in leasing property, while others have nightmare stories to relate.

4. Federal Zone Concession

The Federal Zone applies to beachfront properties. The Mexican federal government owns 20 meters or about 66 feet of the high tide line under the Federal Maritime Land Zone Law. It is possible for foreigners and Mexicans to obtain use of the beach land for a reasonable fee under a concession granted by the federal government. The concession grants temporary use and at the option of the government, these concessions may be renewed for specific periods of time. The fees depend on the specific use of that portion of the property. For instance, if you garden and landscape that part of the property, there may be no charge. If you have your deck or patio in a Federal Zone, it may be something like $50 per month. If all or part of your house is in the Federal Zone, it will be higher. Be careful about buying a home that is entirely in the Zone. If you have as much as 10 feet of the house in a bank trust and you obtain the balance in a concession, then you are covered. These concessions give you the right to enjoy the land and no one can come to build a taco stand in front of you. Don't assume these concession rights run with the land. In 95% of the cases, the government will not allow a transfer of the right. Read the current paperwork. If a reversionary clause exists, the concession reverts automatically back to the government upon sale of the property. If the grant is in the name of a corporation that is sold with the property, the concession will automatically transfer with the corporation because it will remain in the corporation name.

Note: It's wise to obtain a concession if your land is adjacent to the Federal Zone even if you never intend to use it, because anyone else who owns adjacent land could usurp your right by obtaining it for themselves. They could then

298 · BAJA FOR YOU

do what they wish with the land whether you like it or not. A hot dog stand, a horse rental business or a large building could block your view and make your life miserable. Even if it presently wouldn't bother you, it would certainly have an impact in the future on the resale value of your property. The concession will protect your rights. Get it!

What are the duties of a Mexican notary?

The Mexican notary is quite different from the notaries in the United States. In the United States a notary can be anyone who works as a secretary, bank officer, etc. In Mexico the notary is a public official appointed by the State Governor. He has the capacity to attest and certify documents and business and legal transactions that require authenticity. He provides for strict security of original records and documents. To become a Mexican notary one must:

♦ be a Mexican citizen

♦ be at least 35 years of age

♦ have a law degree

♦ have three years experience working in a notary office

♦ take and pass an examination

If he passes, in time, the Governor will give him an appointment.

In Mexico, all legal documents such as deeds, wills, power of attorneys, establishment of legal trusts and other legal transactions must be made before a notary in order to be valid. It is the notary who will oversee the closing of a real estate transaction.

The notary will need the following from each party to a home purchase: proof of full name, proof of date and place of birth, official identification with a photograph, such as a passport or driver's license, and proof that you are in Mexico legally.

When looking for a property should I use a real estate agent to help me?

When trying to find a property in Mexico, it's wise to ask for a reputable real estate agent's assistance. A professional agent will understand the area and will save you from making costly errors. There are homes for sale in areas that are under legal disputes; there are condominiums that are so poorly constructed that the cupboards fall off the wall and there are other questions that only an agent would know to ask. When you first make contact with an agent, be certain to tell her/him what you're looking for. Include the desired price range, size, location, number of bedrooms as well as the style. Do you want to live on the waterfront, a hill or in town? Do you want to buy a resale home or would you prefer to find a lot on which to build your dream home? Instead of having to suffer through a tour of everything on the market, the agent can show you selections that match your description and thus consolidate time. Don't expect to find a waterfront house for $30,000 in Northern Baja California, Mexico, unless you desire a manufactured home on leased land. A good agent may advise you to rent in the area for a time before you make an investment.

Is it possible to get title insurance on property in Mexico?

Yes. Obtaining title insurance is an American business practice, not a Mexican one. It is now possible to get it in Mexico but the property has to meet certain criteria and it will add costly fees to the transaction. However, the peace of mind it offers may be well worth the time, effort and cost. The following companies have a central location in Mexico. They will ask for the paperwork to be sent to them for approval, thus adding time onto the wait for the transaction to close.

Under Mexican insurance law, it is illegal for a Mexican entity, person or company to purchase offshore insurance policies if they are available in Mexico. Be certain the company you use is licensed to do business in Mexico. The following companies are available:

The Settlement Company—Located in Cabo, they offer services anywhere in Mexico. Call 011-52-114-2-20-06. E-mail: info@settlement-co.com

Title Insurance de Mexico—This company created an alliance between Mexico's oldest insurance company, Grupo Nacional Provincial and Chicago Title Insurance Company. Their title insurance policies are the first and only policies registered with and approved by the Mexican Insurance Commission. TIM offers two types of Owner and Loan policies: a standard Mexican policy and a U.S. policy modeled after and containing the same basic coverages as the American Land Title Association ("ALTA") policy form including a direct access endorsement to Chicago Title in the US. Both types of policies insure commercial and residential properties throughout Mexico, including beachfront and border properties (excluded zones), issued in either US dollars or Mexican pesos and can be written to insure any recognized land interest in Mexico including direct ownership, leasehold and trust or beneficial ownership (*fideicomiso*). Among the risks against which the insured is protected are the following:

♦ mortgages

♦ mechanic's and/or tax liens

♦ easements

♦ contractual obligations restricting the use of the property

♦ adverse possession by a third party

♦ agrarian (*ejido*) matters

For further information contact David Wiesley at 1-800-454-1997; (214) 720-0031; (214) 720-4038 fax; dwiesley@titlemex.com or visit their web page at www.titlemex.com

What paperwork will be required in order to obtain title insurance?

Title Insurance De Mexico requires the following paperwork which the seller or your Mexican lawyer can supply:

♦ Property's Deed of Title or conveyance, or the **Escritura**.

♦ Contract or agreement of sale or mortgage information, or **Contrado de Compraventa**.

Other paperwork requested may include:

♦ Bank appraisal, no older than three months, or **Avalua Bancario**.

- Certificate of absence and/or existence of liens, no older than 30 days, issued by corresponding Public Registry of Property, or *Certificado de Libertad de Gravamenes*.

- Copy of any Preventive Notice filed with the corresponding Public Property Registry by a *Notario Publico*, freezing the Property's file, or *Aviso Preventivo al Registro Publico de la Propiedad*.

- Certificate of water and tax payments and extraordinary contributions made to the municipal tax authority, or *Certificado de no adeudo a la Tesoreria local*.

- Water payment receipts and extraordinary contributions made to municipal tax authority, or *Recibos de agua*.

- Property tax receipts for the last five years, or *Boletas prediles*.

- Existing mortgage or Deed of Trust or mortgage cancellation letter or release from the previous mortgage holder, or *Escritura de Hipoteca o Escritura de cancelacion de hipoteca*.

- Copies of marriage licenses for both buyer and seller, if individuals, or *Copias de acta de matrimonio*.

- General personal information of seller and buyer, including respective spouses if individuals, or corporate information if a corporation or *sociedad anonima*, or *Datos generales del vendedor y comprador o informacion corporativa*.

- Proof of buyer's and seller's domicile, or *Comprobante de domcillo del vendedor y comprador*.

- Power of Attorney of legal representative for seller and buyer, or *Poder del representante del vendedor y comprador*.

For further information, contact Dave Wiesley at 1-800-454-1997 or E-mail: dwiesley@titlemex.com

What real estate terms should I know?

♦ *Avaluo bancario*—bank appraisal

♦ *Bienes raices*—real estate

♦ *Contracto de compraventa*—sale agreement—called earnest money agreement in the States.

♦ *Certicado de libertad de gravamentes*—certificate of absence or existence of liens

♦ *Certificado de no adeudo a la tesoreria local*—certificate of water and tax payments

♦ *Cesion*—assignment of rights

♦ *Derechos*—rights

♦ *Escritura*—public deed of conveyance

♦ *Estudio topografico*—plat map or survey map

♦ *Factura*—receipt

♦ *Fideicomiso*—trust agreement

♦ *Garantia*—guarantee

♦ *Gravame*—lien

♦ *Honorarios*—service fees, commissions etc.

♦ *Impuesto*—tax

♦ *Inscripcion*—recording public record

- *Notario publico*—lawyer who records paperwork for government

- *Predial*—property tax

- *Prima*—money paid for insurance policy

- *Registro publico*—public land registry

- *Zona restringida*—also called the "restricted zone"—100 kilometers (approx. 62 miles) from the borders and 50 kilometers (approx. 31 miles) along the Mexican coastline where foreigners can't take direct title to the land.

Is a US mortgage available in Mexico?

Traditionally, it has been necessary to purchase properties in Mexico for all cash. If a person wanted a home for $100,000, he would have to have $100,000 in cash in order to purchase it. However, since the 1993 NAFTA took effect, US financial institutions have offered mortgages on some Mexican properties. It's now possible to place a down payment on a mortgage rather than having to produce a full price cash payoff. There are now competitive mortgage companies who offer loans on qualifying properties. Don't be surprised if the interest rates as well as the loan fees are higher than those in the United States. The following companies have a presence in Northern Baja California, Mexico:

- **Metrociti Mortgage Company**—based in California, the phone number is: 888-860-0606 ext. 308 or 309.

- **Inland Mortgage Company**—phone number: 1-800-585-1984 or 001-800-545-4870 ext 8203 or 8507.

♦ **D.P. Consulting Services Inc.** for commercial development or construction loans for up to $75 million. Call Vincent Fuller at (612) 529-4992.

♦ **Golden Shores Financial**—(949) 661-7636. Ask for Michael Huber.

Generally, the following limitations apply:

♦ Property type—vacation or second home in resort area. Time shares not acceptable.
♦ No bankruptcy or foreclosures for purchaser within the last seven years.
♦ No judgment or liens against borrower.

Over time lending institutions will make it easier to obtain loans, but these are the "pioneer companies" which have entered into the Mexican markets. Remember, not too long ago it was totally impossible to get a loan in Mexico. "All cash" at closing is still the easiest method of payment, but it always has been, even in the United States.

Describe a Mexican home.

Mexicans prefer to live on the hills that provide an expansive vista of the ocean, while the Americans prefer to live right on the water's edge. Mexicans understand the corrosion and upkeep that is caused by the wet, salty air near the ocean. A Mexican kitchen will not necessarily be as big as an American kitchen, nor will it have a view because the housekeeper spends more time in it than does the lady of the house. Mexican homes will have a cozy area for the family to gather to watch television or to play games together. A Mexican home will be secured with an outside wall around a courtyard in order to keep the family safely within and intruders outside.

What is the *Ejido*?

The *Ejidos* are a community of local farmers who were granted over 10,000 acres of land in 1930 by General Lazaro Cardenas, President of Mexico at that time. Recently, the *Ejidos* in Rosarito have been trying to claim some land that others occupy. A cloud has been placed on titles and lawsuits are in progress to settle disputes. When considering purchasing property it is wise to ask if it's *Ejido* land and/or if there's a cloud over the title. There's a certain strip of land that falls under this dispute. Find out where it is and proceed with caution. If it's owned by *Ejido* with no cloud, there could still be a delay in obtaining proper paperwork from Mexico City. Many don't like to bother with this type of land. Let wisdom, not fear influence your decision.

What should I know about building a new home in Mexico?

Many choose to build their dream home in order to get exactly what they want for location, size, design and colors. It could be less expensive than resale homes but building could be a negative experience if not handled correctly. Do research. Talk to local residents who have built new homes. Ask them what they would have done differently. It's wise to be cautious about building because there are many nightmare stories told by people who have built homes in Mexico. Read the book, *God and Mr. Gomez* by Jack Smith which describes his adventure of building a house in Baja

California. Conditions have changed dramatically since he wrote his book, but his descriptions are well written and quite entertaining. You'll enjoy his story.

Consider the following:

♦ When the land is identified, make the offer contingent upon water, electricity, septic or sewer availability, and verify that the land can be legally sold and that the owner has a saleable deed. Search as far back as possible into the recorded line of ownership so someone else doesn't appear as the owner at some other date. In Mexico, centralization of records is not the same as in the States.

♦ Make certain the land isn't made of fill, that erosion is not a factor and check if telephone lines are available. If you decide to build on leased land, understand that if you build you could eventually lose all the money you invest in improvements when the lease is over. A land lease for more than a ten-year period is illegal.

♦ With a credible Mexican lawyer, create a contract to be signed by the builder that protects you in all aspects of the job. To be legal, any contract in Mexico must be written in Spanish. Also have signed copies in English.

♦ Use only dependable and experienced architects, contractors, and construction companies who have been highly recommended and trained. Don't go for those who offer the cheapest rates. Remember, "you get what you pay for."

♦ Ask to go through homes the above people have built or designed.

♦ Architect's design will be created based on size, style, rooms and features you desire.

♦ Permits and blueprints are to be created by the architect, then approved and registered with the government.

♦ List the specifications, materials and budget to be approved by you. Work out a "pay as you complete" funds disbursement schedule that is suitable for you as well as for the architect/builder.

♦ Give architect/builder a reasonable time to complete work, such as six months. Have him agree to pay you $100 a day or more for each day of delay past the agreed-upon completion date.

What are specific problems I could encounter while building my home?

♦ Think about your lifestyle. Where will most of the time be spent? Make the rooms conform to your habits and desires.

♦ Quality of materials—carefully select the materials used. Many Americans think that because a home is built with wood frame and insulation in the United States, it would be suitable construction by the ocean in Mexico. When a person brags about possessing a house built in the American style, my radar antenna goes crazy. The philosophy of "When in Mexico do as the Mexicans do," should be applied. There are excellent Mexican architects/builders who are equal to the best in the United States. Drive past the custom-built Mexican *haciendas* on the hills. Then study the effects on lumber when it's constantly exposed to the moisture and salt air in an ocean climate. Mexicans build with concrete block construction for many reasons. Find out what those reasons are. Be aware there are certain moisture seepage compounds that need to be applied prior to the final stucco or paint on concrete block homes.

♦ Check that windows are adequately placed so that water will run away from the house, not into it. Another common mistake is that sliding glass doors and shower doors are placed backwards so that the track is on the outside rather than on the inside. Make certain yours is adequately installed.

♦ Consider burying a heavy safe in concrete in a camouflaged manner while the house is being constructed. Also, plan a solid protective enclosure around the house. Make it secure from outside invasion. Study the Mexican plans for this protection.

♦ Utilize all possible storage areas. Don't allow spaces to be sealed off if they could possibly be used.

♦ Be certain the plan allows for adequately sized windows that take advantage of the view. I've seen many new homes with a fireplace located where a window should be.

♦ Have a plan for placement of electrical outlets. It's easy to forget to put them on a fireplace mantle, or outside for Christmas or patio lights or in places you want to hang pictures. Make certain the wiring is completed in the early stages of construction, not during the finishing stage.

♦ Adequate outside faucets for watering plants or in a garage for car-washing are sometimes forgotten.

♦ One lawyer created a fireproof room off his garage so he could store his files and important papers. The locks are similar to ones installed on a safe. He also put a phone line in it so messages and faxes could be privately sent while he was away. The maid or others who may be staying in his home can't touch his messages or faxes.

- Pre-wire the house for phone lines, cable TV, security systems and stereos. Be aware that if more than one telephone wire is installed, the wires must be made of a certain component that won't send crossover sounds. If you need multiple lines, check out this important fact before making mistakes. Plastic tube casing for the wiring should be used to avoid rust and corrosion.

- Metal will rust quickly by the ocean, so any time plastic can be installed, such as for fuse boxes, electrical plugs, screens, or light fixtures, use it. Avoid metals at all costs!

- If wood is used, make certain it is treated for bug and water resistance. If cement is used, check on the quality of the mixture. Do adequate research.

- Know that drainage pipes are adequate. One person had constant trouble with sewage flow because his house was built lower than the street pipes. Another found that her house was directly in the path of a stream caused by winter water runoff from nearby hills. Still another has an area for his propane tank that is too small for a new tank to fit, so he is unable to replace his old tank with a larger new tank.

- Constantly check on the progress of the work. Don't be afraid to stop the work in order to correct a mistake. If you deviate from the original plans, ask the architect/builder to sign a **change order form** at the time the change is made. Include a cost estimate on these forms so no confusion will occur when a bill is presented.

- Don't hesitate to change workers if you feel the quality of construction is suffering. Consider paying an extra day's wages to get rid of poor workers. It's wise to maintain good public relations.

- Don't alienate your architect/builder with a bossy or demanding attitude. Remember to be polite in all your dealings.

- Don't build unless you have time to do the necessary homework and checkups on the quality of construction. Don't choose an architect/builder for his cheap bid. Go for quality. Remember, "you get what you pay for."

When purchasing property in Mexico what questions should I ask?

Keep in mind the old saying, *caveat emptor* or "buyer beware". Don't let the Baja bug bite you so hard that you leave your brains at home and make decisions based on emotions. Don't be afraid to purchase in Mexico, just do your homework! You can avoid mistakes others have made by being knowledgeable. Use reasoning to find satisfactory answers for the following questions about the property:

- Be aware that real estate agents do not have to be licensed in Mexico. Make certain the one you use is reputable, professional and knowledgeable. Do not buy property without adequate representation. It may be wise to hire an attorney.

- Make certain the seller holds the deed for the property and has the right to sell it. Deed problems are rampant in Mexico. Many times they are exchanged from family member to family member without government recordings. This is called a *puesta nombre*. (See page 300 about title insurance.)

- Make certain to close with a *notario* who checks records not only in the town in which the property exists but in nearby towns as well. There have been cases where Mr. X sold property in 1950 to Mr. Y. Both Mr. Y and Mr. X have since died. This transaction was recorded in Rosarito, the town in which the property existed. But Mr. X's son showed the deed his father had prior to 1950 to a buyer, convincing the buyer he had title, but he insisted upon closing it in Ensenada instead of in Rosarito where the deed showed ownership by Mr. Y. The notario failed to check the records in Rosarito when the sale closed. Mr. Y's children have to take this case to court to settle the dispute.

♦ How long will I have to wait for the closing to take place? Expect it to take twice as long as in the States, especially if a bank trust is formed. Be flexible. Remember, this is Mexico. Time is not of the essence.

♦ What are all the fees and expenses in purchasing the property? Will they be higher than in the States? Fees will increase accordingly if a loan is issued or if a bank trust is needed. Get original receipts for all expenses and keep them for tax purposes.

♦ Is there an existing bank trust on the property? Is it an individual trust or a master trust? In order to form a new trust, you will need to have your FM-3 in place. Consider putting the property in the name of a corporation or family trust in order to shield your individual liability.

Note: If the corporation is a sole entity, the next purchaser can buy the corporation, thereby eliminating the necessity of government recording. Hence, Mexican capital gains taxes can be avoided. See a lawyer.

♦ Check the location of the property thoroughly. Is it near vacant property that will someday be a fish factory or something that can adversely effect the value?

♦ Is it *Ejido* land? If it is, beware of problems. Do not purchase it on promises of clear title. Get expert legal advice.

♦ If it's in a subdivision, what are the restrictions as written in the CCRs or formal paperwork? Are they enforced? How? What are the homeowner monthly dues? What is the percentage of delinquent monthly payments? Ask for an accounting statement of assets and liabilities or plans to increase the payments. What is the history of the subdivision?

♦ Are there any liens on the property? The *notario* will do a search for official liens before closing, but have the owner sign a document verifying there are no unrecorded liens and that if any appear at any time, he will be responsible for them.

♦ Are property taxes current? Ask to see the original receipts for the last five years. Get copies for your file.

♦ There are no home inspectors in Mexico, so you will want a thorough inspection to be done by a qualified builder. Just as in the States, make the offer contingent upon your approval of an inspection by a person of your choice. Then ask for proper repairs on the items to be fixed. Make certain they are completed before you sign the final paperwork. Your signature on the final papers will be the only leverage you will have to get it finished. Do not sign final papers just on promises of completion. You will be the loser.

♦ Make certain the property is not built on landfill. A professional geological engineer can answer erosion concerns. Pay for an inspection, especially on waterfront property. It's wise to know what you are purchasing.

♦ Ask to see the original water bill receipts covering the

previous five-year period and include copies in your files. Know the water source for the property and have the water tested for purity by a reputable company.

- Know about the septic or sewage system. Is there a treatment facility in the subdivision? Can the land pass a perc test for a septic system? Where does the waste go? How well does the system work in the house? Is the house lower than the drainage pipes? Is a pump used?

- Be certain to check that the utilities are connected to the proper meters.

- Are there telephone connections available? How much will it cost to connect? How long will it take to connect?

- What fire protection is available? How close is the nearest fire department? If it takes the fire department an hour to get to the property, you need to know that fact.

- Is there security on the property? Lights, dogs, guards or fence around the property? When was the last break-in?

- What is the history of the house? Have there been deaths or illnesses or drugs in it?

- If the house is sold completely furnished, make an inventory list of every item you want and have the seller initial every item. I know of a case where the real estate agent took the most valued antiques before turning over the keys to the buyer.

- If the house is on the waterfront, it's very important to know where the Federal Zone ends. Is any part of the house in the Federal Zone? Did the owner obtain a concession? If so, don't assume it runs with the land or that you'll be able to obtain a new one. Don't assume anything! Remember, it's the government that grants it, not the current owner of the property. Read the paper work and find out costs and procedures from a knowledgeable representative before you sign on the dotted line.

What facts should I consider when selling my property in Mexico?

♦ A capital gains tax is to be paid by the seller. Check with a tax lawyer to find out if you qualify for exemptions that could save you money. The appraisal of the house will play a role in the taxes as will whether or not you have lived in it for the last five years. All the *facturas* or receipts showing acquisition, improvement and expense costs will be necessary to calculate and prove what your tax liability will be.

♦ Do you have a recorded deed? Or a bank trust? A bank trust will make your house more saleable to Americans. If you have any title problems, get them straightened out before the house is on the market.

♦ Avoid carrying papers for a private contract, if possible. It's very difficult to get someone out of the house once they're in it. Become knowledgeable about adverse possession laws.

♦ Fix your house up by getting rid of clutter and painting where it needs it.

♦ Make it available for as many showings as possible.

♦ Allow a sign to be placed on your home. It's an effective way to advertise.

When I sign the paperwork, what do I need to do?

♦ Do not sign any papers that you have not read thoroughly. Make certain the English translations match the Spanish meaning.

♦ If the paperwork isn't drafted in Spanish, it will not be honored in a Mexican court of law.

♦ Original signatures are needed on all paperwork. Copies are not honored in a Mexican court of law. Make certain the copy you have in your possession is original.

♦ If the following words are in the contract, don't sign the paperwork without full knowledge of the consequences: "Buyer shall forfeit his/her investment and the **contract shall be voided if** . . ."

♦ Don't sign paperwork with a *Coridor Publico*—This is a person who buys and transfers personal property like a *Notario Publico* but he is not a government official as is a *Notario Publico*.

What closing costs should I expect in Mexico?

Generally, you should expect your closing costs for a cash purchase of a property to be approximately 3-5% of the purchase price. If you obtain a loan, you can figure on an additional 3%. Title insurance, which is not available to all properties, will add another costly fee.

♦ Trustee Fees (bank trust fees): percentage of value set-up fee, $350-$500 annual fee

♦ Foreign Affairs Ministry Permit: $850

- *Notario* Fees: Between .25%-3% of the value
- Recording/Inscription Fees: 1%
- Tax Assessment Appraisal: Varies by area
- Transfer Tax: 2% of property value
- Apostille Fee: Varies by area (approx. $50)

What is the procedure for moving household goods and furniture into Mexico?

When you have obtained your FM-3 visa, you are entitled to a one-time opportunity to bring goods into Mexico without the cost of an import tax. TV and electronic equipment, at least a year old, may be included.

A detailed list in both English and Spanish must include the brand, model and serial numbers of all electrical equipment. Be certain it is typewritten without any spaces between the lines and that each page is signed at the bottom. Make at least three copies of it, one to be saved for your own records. The list should be as brief as possible. For example: 5 boxes of linens, 13 boxes of dishes, 1 kitchen table, etc.

Consult with the nearest Mexican consulate for advice and current price of the permit (approximately $75 at the time of this writing). Bring a money order or cashier's check when you apply.

You may want to hire a customs broker to handle the load through customs since there can be disparities on what the consulate considers "free" and what the individual agent at the border will interpret.

318 · BAJA FOR YOU

What is the procedure for moving my goods back into the United States?

United States customs will charge $20 for crossing the border into the US. The list of your goods, a copy of your ID and the address of the destination of the goods is needed.

What moving companies can handle my move from the States to Baja California, Mexico?

Many residents report a successful experience with the following moving company:

International Moving, Alberto Jaramillo. "We can move your household goods safely and securely with all permits and insurance. USA to Mexico; Mexico to the USA." Call for free estimate: (011-52-66) 12-1342 or (619) 595-7363.

If we use a US moving company, will they be able to cross the border?

Only those companies with a branch in Mexico can get across the border. Some people will have a US moving company bring their goods to a storage unit in Chula Vista or San Ysidro. They will then transfer the goods into a Mexican truck to head across the border or they will store the load in a storage unit until they're ready for it to be delivered in Mexico. Sometimes people will bring one box at a time across the border into Mexico.

Where can I store my goods close to the border until I find a place to live?

A **Storage Place** in Chula Vista has an on-site manager, closed circuit TV and has individually lighted spaces, as well as RV spaces and business storage. The address is 605 Anita St. (Off-Broadway). Call (619) 425-8222.

If I invest money in Mexico for a home, will it be a secure investment?

If you make a wise choice when you purchase, preferably under the advisement of a reliable real estate agent, your investment is never guaranteed, as in the States. If a buyer wants to buy and a seller wants to sell, the price they negotiate to satisfy both parties becomes the sales price. An appraiser looks at sales prices of comparable homes within the last six months. These sales prices determine the current market value. As long as there are buyers who are willing to pay the price, the market holds. When a buyer pays more for a property, the value goes up. If there are no buyers and the seller lowers the price, values go down. In a subdivision in Baja California where the most likely buyers are US citizens, the value of an existing house is dependent on the value of the dollar or the psychological mind set of the purchaser. If the dollar is strong and the purchaser wants to buy, property values remain stable. However, if the peso significantly devalues when a home is being built by a Mexican developer/builder who is dependent upon the peso, a buyer can be hurt. Promised amenities may not be forthcoming. The worst scenario is a bankruptcy and foreclosure of the property before a bank trust is placed in the purchaser's name. Most builders/developers are Mexican who are most likely dependent upon the value of the peso, so it becomes crucial to check the financial backing of those you hire. Remember the words *caveat emptor* or "buyer beware." Prudence and wisdom are necessary in all real estate transactions.

Why is this a wise time to purchase property in Northern Baja California?

All the economic signs indicate an upswing in the real estate market. After a long period of downward stagnation, the California real estate market has regenerated itself in an upward spiral. Confidence in the economy is enhanced by low interest rates. The Baja California Mexican market is starting to feel the same increase and will probably continue to rise in a trickle down effect within a year. It is a transitional time because sellers perceive it to be a buyer's market. In order for a purchase to occur, a seller has to want to sell and a buyer has to want to buy. The psychological perception of each will determine the outcome of the negotiations. Recently multiple offers for a single property are renewing confidence in sellers and hence, driving the prices upward. If this trend continues, values will rise and appreciation is inevitable.

Why is the Baja California real estate market so dependent on the success of the California-US market?

Rosarito, Baja California, is within a 20-minute commute of the California-Mexico border. Rosarito has traditionally been a beach-resort town offering rest and relaxation to holiday tourists. Because of the close proximity, Californians travel with ease back and forth between countries.

Do buyers come from other areas as well?

The majority of real estate buyers have traditionally been Californians; however with easy Internet access, the entire world is starting to investigate the potential of the area. For example, a Michigan buyer found an advertisement on the Internet for a beachfront condominium project. The pictures were enticing enough to stimulate him to travel to Baja California to investigate this project further. He's now awaiting a new home to be built on the ocean for a fraction of the price he would have had to pay in the States.

Nevada or Arizona residents enjoy Baja California in the summer to get away from the heat, while Oregon residents seek a relief from the rain. Canadians love the temperate climate and everyone takes advantage of the reasonable cost of living.

How do Mexicans feel about the influx of Americans to their country?

Economically it has caused the area to have very little, if any, unemployment problems. Rosarito boasts of the lowest unemployment rate in all of Mexico. The Secretary of Tourism spends a lot of money advertising to draw US citizens to the area. Houses, condominiums and services are constantly being constructed to accommodate the needs of the influx of people. The Mexican government has very strict laws that protect its citizens against losing employment to foreigners. Thus a balance is struck between encouraging tourism and protecting local employment.

What general economic influences will bring Americans to Baja California?

Current US tax laws allow a home owner to sell a primary residence without having to pay a capital gains tax on an increase of up to $500,000 a couple or $250,000 per person. Buying a more expensive home and rolling over the proceeds is no longer necessary. The possibility of purchasing a less expensive home is now an option.

As Americans search for options, they will find the cost of living in Baja California to be favorable to their budgets. The number of retirees will continue to escalate as the generation of Baby Boomers consider retirement and eventually reach retirement age. Baja California will capture the hearts of many as they consider the proximity to the States, perfect weather and reasonable economy. They will find a place that maximizes an enjoyable way of life while minimizing the cost of living.

NAFTA has opened up trade between countries. As mentioned earlier, many companies have chosen to invest in Baja California. Costco Price Club and Marriott Hotels have a presence here and are planning expansions. With increased services, life in Baja California becomes more attractive to those not wanting to give up the amenities of the United States.

AFTERWORD

Adiós mis amigos!

I hope you have gleaned much information from this book. Please offer feedback, especially if you have experiences that need to be included in future editions. Remember Roberta as your friend in Northern Baja, California. You may request me if you need a speaker for a seminar or meeting. Order this book for educational training, gifts or fund raising. Quantity discounts are available for bulk purchases.

♦ URL: http://www.baja4u.com

♦ E-mail: baja4u@hotmail.com

♦ Call:1-888-9BAJA4U (225248)

♦ Write:

ScriptStone Publishing Inc.,
2675 Windmill Parkway, #612
Henderson, NV 89014

INDEX

Tijuana Open-Air Market—Find the treasure of your choice at this Tijuana open-air market. Bartering is accepted and enjoyed, especially on Sunday.

La Misión—The majesty of the Pacific Ocean commands awe and respect from those who view this typical site in Baja California, Mexico.

PHOTO JOURNAL OF BAJA CALIFORNIA

Enjoy the charm and beauty of Baja California, Mexico. Be careful. The Pacific Ocean, the sunsets and the people will captivate your heart.

How would you like to have a backyard with this view? The Pacific Ocean is enjoyed by the residents of this **San Antonio Del Mar** location. The stunning sunsets are normal, especially on this December day.

Popotla is a little fishing village within Rosarito which offers fresh fish to local residents. Nearby Twentieth Century Fox Studios produced *The Titanic* and other water related movies in this beautiful area of the Pacific Ocean.

Mexican "Fuller Brush" Man—This truck travels the roads to find buyers for mops, brooms, brushes, pails etc. The prices are reasonable.

Casa Rosales—Leave your old jewelry with George Rosales to fashion into something stunningly new, or buy new jewelry for a fraction of US prices. Located on the main street of Rosarito, his shop is rated highly among the locals.

René's Restaurant—Locals meet at René's Restaurant to eat, drink, dance and socialize. Located just South of town in Rosarito, this place dates back to the 1930s when the rich and famous first came to Rosarito Beach.

Dick's Mail Room—US mail is picked up and delivered three times a week at Dick's Mail Room. Located next to Renés Restaurant in Rosarito, it's a popular local gathering place.

The San Ysidro border crossing is one of the most traveled international borders in the world. Being aware of the times of the heaviest traffic flow is crucial to those who have to cross often.

Go through these arches to the **Rosarito Beach Hotel**, a famous Baja California historical landmark. Located on a white sandy beach in downtown Rosarito, this site is a must to visit.

© Elvia Tadeo

This pastel of a mexican hat salesman is an original by **Elvia Tadeo**, a noted member of the La Jolla Art Association who originates from Baja California, Mexico.

Andrés Meling, a well-known Baja California, Mexico vaquero and guide, stands in front of the home in which he was born at the Meling Ranch located in the mountains south of Ensenada.

The **Rosarito fire department** is ready to function at a moment's notice. The firemen are friendly and trained to help in crisis situations.

Club Marena, located on a popular surfing cove at K-38.5, offers luxury condominium living with all the amenities of a first class resort.

ORDER FORM

Make a copy of this form and send to:

ScriptStone Publishing Inc.
2675 Windmill Parkway, #612
Henderson, NV 89014

Book	Quantity	Price	Total
Baja4You	_____	x$19.95=	_____
Get Out of the Rat Race Now	_____	x$18.95=	_____
		subtotal	_____
		State tax	_____
	Postage & Handling $3.95*		_____

only $2 for each additional book

TOTAL _____

Ship To: _____

Name: _____

Company Name: _____

Address: _____

_____ Zip Code: _____

Payment: ☐ Check   ☐ Money Order

Credit Card: ☐ Visa   ☐ Master Card

Card Number: _____ Exp. Date: _____

Name on Card (Print): _____

Signature: _____

**CALL TOLL FREE AND ORDER NOW
1 - 8 8 8 - 9 - b a j a 4 u   (2 2 5 2 4 8)**